THE RAUSCHENBUSCH LECTURESHIP FOUNDATION
OF THE COLGATE-ROCHESTER DIVINITY SCHOOL
ROCHESTER, NEW YORK

THE RAUSCHENBUSCH FOUNDATION was established in March 1929 at the Colgate-Rochester Divinity School in memory of the late Walter Rauschenbusch, illustrious exponent of social Christianity and, from 1902 to 1918, professor of church history in Rochester Theological Seminary, to which institution the Colgate-Rochester Divinity School is successor.

The movement for the establishment of this foundation was initiated by a gift of ten thousand dollars from Mrs. Edmund Lyon, of Rochester, New York, conditioned upon the raising of twenty-five thousand dollars from other sources. An amount somewhat in excess of that sum was secured through the generous gifts of citizens of Rochester, alumni of Rochester Theological Seminary, and others.

The general field of the lectureship is that of Christianity in its social expression and application. A series of lectures upon this foundation is to be given annually during Alumni Week in the Colgate-Rochester Divinity School, these lectures to be published in book form and known as the Rauschenbusch Lectures.

Publications on

THE RAUSCHENBUSCH LECTURESHIP FOUNDATION

THE MORAL CRISIS IN CHRISTIANITY
Justin Wroe Nixon

THE SOCIAL GOSPEL AND THE CHRISTIAN CULTUS
Charles Clayton Morrison

THE SOCIAL TRIUMPH OF THE ANCIENT CHURCH
Shirley Jackson Case

AN INTERPRETATION OF CHRISTIAN ETHICS
Reinhold Niebuhr

BROTHERHOOD ECONOMICS
Toyohiko Kagawa

CHURCH AND STATE IN THE MODERN WORLD
Henry Pitney Van Dusen, et al.

THIS NATION UNDER GOD
Arthur Erastus Holt

THIS NATION . UNDER GOD

" — *that this nation, under God, shall have a new birth of freedom.*" ABRAHAM LINCOLN

THIS NATION UNDER GOD

ARTHUR E. HOLT

Professor of Social Ethics,
Chicago Theological Seminary
and
The Divinity School,
The University of Chicago

WILLETT, CLARK & COMPANY

CHICAGO   NEW YORK

1939

Dedicated

*To those thousands of men
who till the soil and furnish
the cities with pure food, not because
they have to but because they want to,
and in their organized activities
constitute the one hope of
democratic regionalism.*

Contents

FROM THE AUTHOR TO THE READER 1

THE SOIL IN WHICH DEMOCRACY GROWS 5

RESPONSIBLE LIVING IN A DEMOCRACY 10

HOW THE AMERICAN PEOPLE BECAME IRRESPONSIBLE 37

DEMOCRACY'S COMPETITORS 57

CHRISTIANITY AND DEMOCRACY IN THE PRIMARY RE-
LATIONSHIPS OF LIFE 74

CHRISTIANITY AND DEMOCRACY IN THE PUBLIC ORDER 85

THE CHURCH NOURISHING THE ROOTS OF DEMOCRACY 126

THE CHURCH IN SOCIAL EDUCATION AND SOCIAL AC-
TION 153

WORSHIP AS BASIC SELF-DIRECTION 181

Acknowledgments

Through the courtesy of the Colgate-Rochester Theological Seminary, I was asked to deliver the Rauschenbusch Lectures for 1938. Some of the material included in these lectures I have used in *Christendom* and also in a book, published by the Pilgrim Press, entitled *The Church and Social Work,* and in another book, published by the Association Press, entitled *The Bible as a Community Book.* All this material is now out of print, but I wish to acknowledge my indebtedness to the Pilgrim Press and to the Association Press for the privilege of reusing it.

I am greatly indebted to Dr. Anton T. Boisen for the reading of the manuscript and to Miss Margaret Medland for her careful, painstaking work in copying and correcting it.

ARTHUR E. HOLT

THIS NATION UNDER GOD

From the Author to the Reader

We are witnessing a tumultuous search for new communities of responsible living. These new communities may be paternalistic; if so they will fall before some future revolution. Or they can be democratic and become part of the fabric of a society which works for the spiritual maturity of humanity. A part of the road back to responsible living will be the rediscovery of a sense of community which will perform the function that the old simple community performed, but will do it in terms of modern life. Manifestly it is neither possible nor profitable to return to the early economy of home production and neighborhood consumption. The community of the future must deal with a world of railroads, steamships, labor unions and employers' associations, professional men and farmers.

In the United States there have been two partial expressions of the community idea: first, a naive belief in the old simple type of community, which once was effective, wherein public opinion and mores temper the enthusiasms of the individual person or group; second, an attitude which sees the government, local, state or federal as the symbol of community. The small face-to-face community is the natural school for the learning of the meaning of responsible conduct. It is here that the early images of life are formed in the mind. When people cease to live in families and villages they will find it increasingly hard to have a picture of God as a father and of other human beings as brothers. The government as the symbol of community has its drawbacks. The popular belief has been that that government is best which governs least. The total result of this theory is resentment of all interference on the part of the government which seems to limit individual and group freedom. If the community was represented by the government the community had to be very inarticulate since, under the doctrine of laissez faire, we were taught that, if the individual and each group sought its own welfare, the public welfare was served. That is a very inadequate idea, as we are rapidly learning.

In between the small community and community as represented by the government, there was very little social control of a large share of American life. The professions carried on with an eye to their own prestige and development. The great class-conscious groups of traders, farmers, laborers and consumers considered themselves social ultimates and there was no overarching unit which made them all conscious that they existed for something besides themselves. The city was an aggregation of self-seeking groups and there was no larger community which must be served if the economic body was to be full of health.

Now it is just the recovery of a sense of community in these areas which is the problem of responsible living at the present time. We have moved out beyond the social control of the small community. We are represented only in the field of government in this larger area. The tremendous enthusiasm with which people are turning to the state grows out of the popular belief that the state is this larger community which has the right to control all the lesser parts. The state, then, takes control in culture, in the professions, in the vocations; ultimately it must take control of life in the cities; and so you have the formula for a totalitarian state. Unless we can discover a type of community which carries with it a certain moral authority and which can temper man's hunger for prestige and power in the professions and in the field of economics, we will have to accept the state as our ultimate community and allow it to regiment our lives.

Let us frankly affirm that the organization of farmer, laborer and consumer into their relative groups is to be encouraged. There can be no ethics without power, and power must return to the disinherited and power must be taken from those who have appropriated more than their share of it. We cannot go on in a trader-controlled world.

There are those who would solve the problem by taking power away from all industrial groups and transferring it to the government. So far as power is concerned the government would add to its political power the economic power of farmer, laborer, trader and consumer. Here is the adolescent stage of the totalitarian state.

Democracy has not given us an organic society; it has given us an atomistic society full of cleavages. It has not given us a just society; its privileges have been laid at the feet of the capitalist class. Democracy boasts of freedom of speech, freedom of the press and freedom of the pulpit, but these slogans often hide an indefensible selfishness and a bondage which can be easily exposed. The question whether democracy will survive seems to hinge on whether the values of democracy can be maintained while we achieve some fellowship of functions which represent both freedom and that organic quality which society must have, without accepting the state as the instrument of this organic life.

Christianity, with its concern for ultimate spiritual growth on the part of human beings, views this modern struggle for power and it cannot refrain from asking: " Which one of these attempts at community building has a concern for the spiritual growth of the individual and seems most likely to give us a social order whose cohesion is based on social faith and trust? " It cannot lose sight of the ineffectiveness of democracy in dealing with questions of economic justice. It cannot be blind to the hypocrisies of so-called freedom, but it also faces the fact that totalitarian states leave very small opportunity for the exercise of independence and the use of the imagination on the part of common man. It will see that the task of democracy is to believe that people can be loyal to self-chosen goals and can be held together by a trust and a love which are more compelling than force or fear.

The Soil in which Democracy Grows

If you cross the Rio Grande river into Mexico and start traveling south, you will have at your back the two largest countries in the western hemisphere which profess a belief in democracy, and you will travel far before you come to another. If democracy means freedom of function and mutual cooperation among church, state, school and business, Mexico knows little of it. If democracy means that the gains of a commonwealth are mass gains and are to be shared by all in the nation, you will not find it in the semi-feudal, fascist-tending commonwealths of the South American continent. Underneath the white populations which possess the power in South America there is an inarticulate, ancient civilization which has not advanced very much beyond the primitive tribal life in which the white man discovered it. Democracy is an empty word so far as South America is concerned, and one need not be surprised that new forms of government, which do not feel under any obligation to keep up the pretensions of a democratic ideology, are coming into being on that continent.

If you cross from South America to Africa, you will find a gigantic area gripped in the various devices of European and colonial control. A comparatively small number of white men, backed by the armies of the homeland and assisted by government-owned railroads and industries, hold in a tight industrial and agricultural peonage millions of natives who can no longer call the Dark Continent their own. Africa makes no pretensions in the direction of democracy.

Crossing from Africa to Asia you will come upon an ancient caste system thinly overlaid by a veneer of Western imperialistic capitalism, neither of which professes to be democratic. There is much to be said for the ancient caste system which, in both India and China, puts the scholar at the top and gives him the highest award because of his supposed creative ability. But democracy, if it calls for equal opportunity for every man, is not discoverable in the Orient. Nor does Japan, which at the moment seems the Orient's leading nation, make any pretensions in this direction.

If you turn back to Europe, the home of the democracies, you will travel as far west as Switzerland before you come to a country which believes in government of the people, by the people and for the people. Countries like Russia, Germany and Italy challenge the political democracies of the world and insist that all the assumptions of democracy are the outworn slogans of a capitalistic age. The British empire carries on with a modified democracy. It does not democratize social life inside the empire nor has it altogether democratized its economic life. Democracy seems to abide in the countries which developed the democratic way of life when they were small. They are now desperately hanging on to the love of their youth.

Now, without insisting too strongly on the causal relationships, we can discern in these democratic countries certain concomitant relationships which seem to characterize all the countries in which democracy is a success. They are the relationships of people who want to make choices, who take responsibility and seek fellowship. Certain characteristics seem to be common to all countries which successfully maintain democratic government.

The prevailing type of religion in the democratic countries is one which lays a great deal of emphasis on freedom of the individual and relies for unity on fellowship rather than on authority and discipline. Most of the democracies have followed Protestant teachings, which stress education and encourage large investments in schools and colleges. They have brought about a separation of church and state, and have recognized the right of the church to criticize the state and the right of the state to maintain education which criticizes the church. Calvinism teaches that it is good Christianity to criticize the state, and it is interesting to note that none of the Calvinistic countries has accepted the totalitarian state.

A second characteristic of the democratic countries is a certain encouragement for equality of opportunity in economic and social life. However far the democratic countries have departed from the ideal in practice, capitalism originally was born as an attempt to give everyone a chance to take initiative in seeking economic salvation. The democratic countries have encouraged private initiative and then sought to secure for their people new opportunities for economic and social advancement.

A third characteristic of the democratic countries is a certain love for the smaller units of life — the family, the town, the village; in fact, democratic countries were originally the small countries of the world. They have had a distrust of big mass movements. Today they occupy a great part of the earth's surface, but sprawling as they have become in some cases, they are made up largely of self-articulated parts, such as the states of our country or the separate entities of the British empire. Democracy demands for its healthy growth a comprehensible community in which it is possible for the individual to exercise will power, purpose and intelligence over social areas which are close at hand. Such a condition is found in nations where, for one reason or another, there has been a willingness to recognize what has been called " the logic of littleness."

A fourth characteristic of the democratic countries is a fairly consistent refusal to glorify the state and make patriotism a supreme virtue. Their great days of memory and celebration are those which recall occasions when the people rose up and took control of the government.

A fifth characteristic is a respect for truth, which expresses itself in freedom of teaching, freedom of the press, freedom of research. Education is organized around goals which are indigenous to the educational purpose, not around the short-time objectives of some church, class, race or state.

I call these characteristics of democracy, which are so much more than political and really constitute a constellation of super-political factors, the soil in which democracy grows. Democracy is not to be identified with the rural or the urban as such. Its natural soil is neither Tobacco Road nor the Sidewalks of New York. Democracy awaits people who want to make choices, take responsibility and share power through appropriate social institutions; the cry for dictators comes from mobs on the city streets and from disinherited peasants. Democracy is not a political theory which exists by itself. It requires a certain balance among all the functions of life. It cannot be argued or fought or legislated into existence. We lose it when we try to bring it in by war. Shouting drowns it out, and the trappings of parades hide its stalwart virtues. We can have democracy only as we are willing to make it a fact about our total life.

The question then whether you " believe in democracy " is the question whether you believe in a certain set of relationships — spiritual, economic, social and political — actually existing among people in a way that can be called democratic. It is a tribute to the realism of the present world that a very large part of it has ceased to pretend that it professes the creed of democracy, and that a very large number of the professed democracies have recognized that democracy is not just a label you wear on your coat, but a principle which calls for a characteristic organization of all of human life. Therefore, it is not to be entered into hastily or inadvisedly but thoughtfully, prayerfully, and in the fear of God and men.

Responsible Living in a Democracy

Something awful has happened to Christendom. It is more than the paralysis of commerce, though that is a part of it. It is more than industrial debility, which surely is a part of the cataclysm. It is more than political reaction and apathy that chokes and poisons the springs of progress. It is something deeper than the social decadence which is seen in every caste and class and country — the loosening of moral stays and the wilting of ancient standards. The things that are so hopelessly apparent in the realms of business, of industry, of politics, of the social order, are mere symptoms of a spiritual disease. Christendom is sick for lack of Christianity. Faith is dying — faith in men largely. For it is faith that bellies the sails of commerce when the ship goes out; faith that honest men will man her, that honest men will take her cargo, that honest men will send back a decent gain to the owners. It is faith that makes men sweat in industry; faith that their day's work will bring them a decent living, that their day's planning will yield them a good profit. Faith is the centripetal force that holds men together in states, in nations, in associated power; faith that the word of rulers is dependable, faith that the common sense of the people may be trusted to respond to humanity's decent needs under government. Faith holds the home inviolate, and makes the social compact strong and wholesome.

And the Golden Rule, which is the essence of the Christian philosophy, is the basis of faith. But the Golden Rule is badly tarnished today. It has fallen into desuetude. The pessimist, the grouch, the greedy-gut, even the cynic, are expounding the world's current philosophy, and everywhere men are dwelling in fear. The terror of a vast unbelief is gripping mankind in some sort of spiritual glacial epoch, which threatens chaos.[1]

Such a diagnosis would not necessarily apply to a totalitarian state, but it applies with vengeance to a democracy. When Fletcher Dobyns said, " Only a moral revolution can save Chicago," he was stating a very trite but profoundly true fact not only about Chicago but about all democratic civilizations. For democracy is an adventure between the individual and society which assumes that where they are free the individual and the social group can work out through cooperative interplay a satisfying type of common welfare. But that adventure can reach successful consummation only if both the individual and society are responsible to something higher than either. Democracy's one hope of meeting its competitors lies not in a distribution of power — although that may play a part — but in a distribution of moral responsibility whereby the individual unit maintains its right to make a contribution to the total welfare and also accepts its obligation to work for the common welfare.

This peculiar moral quality of democracy becomes clearer by contrast. For instance, the essential difference between Denmark and Germany is that Germany seeks the common welfare through state planning, which is in the hands of the elite and is enforced upon the mass of the people through state agencies of propaganda. Denmark, on the other hand, began with a moral revolution fathered by a young man named Grundtvig. Facing the problem of renewal in his impoverished country, he took as his life slogan: " That which I have lost outwardly I will win inwardly." He felt that moral and spiritual renewal must run ahead of social change. And so he did not seek directly to reconstruct his nation. Instead he established a system of schools in which teachers could speak only the "living word" which would perpetually bring new inward life to the people. Social renewal has followed. A cooperative society, held together not by force and fear but by the social cohesion of faith and trust, has gradually displaced the sterile, autocratic society of Grundtvig's day. Denmark has maintained freedom. Its individual citizens have achieved spiritual maturity, and so common welfare has found adequate and definite expression.

Democracy is also an adventure among the individual social functions such as agriculture, industry, the professions, the church and the state. Here the assumption is that, if each function is separate and free, all will be able to work toward social coordination. From this point of view democracy is essentially an adventure in faith and ethics. Along the highway which connects the different functions of society with one another there must be built up and recognized a system of rights and duties which charts the behavior that guards both freedom and responsibility. Failing this, democracy fails. If one function abuses its freedom all the other functions are tempted to do likewise. The result is chaos.

As one thinks of all the various types of individuals and social functions, each with its tendencies to willfulness, provincialism and inefficiency, one is appalled at the faith of those who believe that the modern world, thrown together by all the techniques of modern communication and transportation, can ever achieve a satisfying type of human welfare. The longing for a dictator, divine or human, who will take off our shoulders the burden of self-government, overwhelms us. Certainly men do not want to stay up nights to keep society running. Yet do any of us really believe that Jehovah will relieve us of the task?

To a greater degree than we are willing to realize, ordinary social change is a matter of moral revolution rather than of social reorganization. Moral attitudes are the foundation upon which freedom and community life rest. There is no new kind of society which does away with the need of integrity and social trust. Integrity is necessary to any kind of achieved freedom. This does not in any way dispense with the need for technical arrangement and well ordered social procedure. They all go together. But basic to all of them is that constellation of attitudes which we are accustomed to classify as moral.

Let us take a very simple illustration. Anyone who ever witnessed one of the old traffic jams in the bottle-neck which once existed at the foot of Michigan boulevard, Chicago, has seen on a small scale an irresponsible mob. In the old horse-and-buggy days the one bridge across the river took care of traffic that did not range very far from its home base. But presently, in place of the horse and buggy there appeared a thousand automobiles each representing twenty horse power and more, all meeting at the old bridge at five o'clock in the afternoon. Furious at the way they obstructed one another they voiced their impatience in human shouts and mechanized screams. Their hysteria grew with their own noise. The powerful became convinced that they must take the responsibility for their own self-preservation and began to crowd the little cars to the wall. Police became gesticulating pygmies submerged in a mass of milling futility. It was chaos in miniature.

To talk about love and mutual aid in this situation seemed like sprinkling eau de cologne on a cage filled with fighting polecats. And yet out of that chaos, an epitome of all traffic jams, orderly procedure *has* emerged, without a return to the horse-and-buggy age. Some of the methods by which we have created order suggest what is involved in the conquering of the world mobs of irresponsible individuals.

There was, first of all, a sense of total involvement. We all wanted to " go places and see things," but since we got into one another's way and fought and destroyed one another we all decided to stay at home. This interdependence, combined with the capacity to sense it, was basic to everything else.

With the growing sense of interdependence came a dislike for the claims of special privilege. We knew that the " road-hog " or the driver who " shot the traffic " started a procedure which could not be universalized, and ultimately defeated not only the rest of us but himself as well. (There may be legitimate claims for special privilege, as on the part of the ambulance or the fire-engine, but such claims have been socialized in advance since their privilege is for the sake of the larger good.)   Adjustment called for a very large amount of individual decision. We took care not to run into this person or that automobile, not because some policeman stood by and told us not to; the driver made his decision and the other person made his decision and they passed without collision, because they were aware of each other. Men are not robots; they are creatures who can anticipate through imagination and therefore have freedom.

The traffic light on the main highway came to be a language which we all understood and increasingly paid attention to. It is a signal which symbolizes our independence and ultimate freedom. (But we want these traffic lights to be located at the main crossings and not in back alleys. Some time ago in a small Virginia village I saw a man and a cow standing in the middle of the street. There was no other traffic in sight. I could not understand why they were standing still until I looked up and noticed that they were waiting for the green light. It was a perfectly good traffic light located at an unimportant crossing.)

Custom played its part in resolving the tangle. We turn to the right. In many other countries traffic turns to the left. This anticipated type of procedure governed by custom also promotes freedom. Again, the engineer, by building underpasses and overpasses, by rounding corners into curves, by placing broad roads where traffic is heaviest, lessened the probability of accident and fostered common welfare. The traffic cop and the law court which dealt with the seeker of special privilege by adjudicating doubtful cases became servants of peace and free procedure.

Thus our traffic jams are resolved into an ordered procedure whereby people may go places and see things without returning to the horse-and-buggy age, because we set up a larger society to which the individual can surrender and find freedom.

Now it is clear that good engineering plays a part in the solution of this problem, that adequate laws and customs and law courts are a part of it; but basic to this transformation is a change of attitude which can be classified only as a moral revolution. There is a new awareness of interdependence. There is a new hatred of special privilege. There is a new sense of consideration for the rights of the other fellow. Even the instrumentalities of law and force rest back upon a perception which makes them instruments of cooperation rather than of compulsion.

❧

If we discern in the fairly simple relationships of good highway procedure the basic necessity for moral and spiritual renewal, how much more do these considerations have weight for the vastly complicated procedures of the whole of society! Democracy was not forbiddingly difficult in the age of homespun when an ever expanding frontier took care of our mistakes, but democracy in today's overpopulated cities is serious business. In the interest of general welfare we have given the ballot to everyone but we have discovered that universal suffrage develops its own kind of predatory conduct. We have had autocracy in industry, and if there is any salvation in control by the elite it should have materialized through the autocratic rule of business or through the city manager system, but these also developed their own type of predatory action. Shift and change social organization as we will and as we must, the fact remains that any kind of system rests back upon a sense of moral values on the part of the population.

The task before us requires all that we can muster of reason, of skill, of courage. It would be the height of futility for us to increase our panic by hysterical screaming about the awfulness of it. Some are more public-minded than others but verbal assassination of fellow sufferers in the midst of an interdependent world is the best preliminary to war and the poorest preparation for peace. It would be equally futile to try to solve our problem by attempting to go back to the age of barter and neighborhood production and consumption. As John Woolman would say, it would seem to be in accordance with the will of God that men should trade and sail the high seas.

If we would save democracy we must first of all recognize the fact of our interdependence. We are in a jam because we cannot escape one another. Since we are interdependent we should search out zealously those seekers of special privilege who will not only destroy this world for others but will ultimately defeat themselves. To declare that this world belongs to the one who asserts most force is false. Such a world arouses not the capacity for large interdependence but evokes more force, and those who live by the sword in the end perish by the sword.

As on the less pretentious highway, individual decision as to what is for the common good will be a very large part of a total program of adjustment. We can avoid collision with the other fellow if we use our imagination and ask what would be good procedure for ourselves if we were in his place. Also, accepted customs which work for orderly procedure on a small scale can be projected into a larger world. There are ways and habits which belong to the good neighbor. Neighborliness is not dependent upon the traffic cop.

Good social engineering which frees and does not restrict this interdependent world will pave the pathway of peace and democracy. Nor is it within reason to believe that business and government can be conducted without a traffic cop and a court. So long as claimants for special privilege will not listen to reason they will have to be eliminated by other methods.

Yet the world that lives by traffic cops and legal procedure has already failed. Nothing other than a moral revolution can save us if we are to carry on as a democracy.

Democracy assumes ideas and attitudes which men hold as they hold their religion. They are great upspringing convictions which root in what one feels about the total cosmic structure.

If there is any value in what is here written it lies in recognition of the fact that the issues of a democratic civilization lie farther back than their institutional expression in family, profession, business organization and the state. This does not mean, as is so often asserted, that there is a personal world which is much more important than the social. No such line between personal and social can be drawn. The institution is a superficial and rather late form of life expression; society is not. The social and the personal are born together. Institutions, while important, come later and are always based on something more fundamental. Democracy as an institutional organization rests back on a conviction about the worth of all individuals and their proper relation to one another. This conviction people hold because of the way they read the great cosmic drama of life. Men die for democracy because they believe that in committing themselves to it they can find the meaning of life and death. Man is never so wonderful as when he takes his readings of the cosmic constants and launches on the great pilgrimage, knowing that sooner or later physical death claims us all. The battle for a world in which there is respect for individuals, where men work together in the unity of common purposes, must be won or lost on the field of those beliefs about man and his cosmic role — beliefs which belong to that constellation of ideas we call religion.

Society does not advance majority-end foremost, but there is good scriptural authority for the statement that prophets come in " schools " and not as single individuals. Three hundred years ago a tight-lipped generation, the merchant seamen of England, started out to conquer the deep. They are the men who lifted that little poverty-stricken island on the west coast of Europe to a dominating place in the world. They did it by adventurous coopera-tion, by charting the heavens and the vast oceans. As a col-lective attack on the hazards of the sea they organized great insurance companies, placed lighthouses on all the impor-tant coasts and charted the ocean currents.

Among them there was a small group who adventured in the name of religion and of a better way of life. They set-tled on the bleak shores of Massachusetts and in the name of God planned and projected a commonwealth. The con-sciousness that they stood in a great historic succession of adventurers in the name of God was like a breeze from the ages filling the sails of the Pilgrim voyagers. To feel this was to believe that there is meaning in history.

In the course of the years another group arrived in Mas-sachusetts. They were not welcomed by the first school of prophets. They were punished, persecuted and legislated against until they had to go to other parts of the country in order to win the chance to live. These people called them-selves Friends and their enemies called them Quakers. From their midst there came, in the latter part of the eight-eenth century, a man by the name of John Woolman. He shared with his fellow Friends certain great, vivid convic-tions. John Woolman meditated upon the world about him and out of his meditations he formulated principles like the following: " True religion consists in an inward life wherein the heart doth love and reverence God the Creator and learns to exercise true justice and goodness not only toward all men but also toward the brute creatures." In accordance with this idea he decided to live simply, without luxury, and to share so far as he could the burdens of his fellows — the dispossessed Indians, the overworked Negro slaves, the sailors who toiled on the high seas. It was a work of the imagination. So successful was he in enlarging the understanding and sympathy of his co-religionists that twenty years after his death the Quakers of the country had voluntarily abolished slavery among themselves.

In a later day a group of young men went forth to take up their homesteads at the foot of the Rocky mountains in what was then known as the Great American Desert. They had a twofold fight on their hands. Nature out there was unfriendly, except to the rattlesnake, the prairie dog and the owl, which were having a fairly good time on the ground that lies east of the Rockies. There was water in the hills and it flowed down the lowest valleys into the Gulf of Mexico. But there was desert on the broad plains. Now the first task of these young men was to redirect the working of nature's forces. Natural law did not specify just which hill water should flow down and there was nothing to hinder water from flowing down the highest hills instead of the lowest valleys if it could find the way. So the young men dug irrigation ditches. They guided the water along the highest hills and let it flow down to vivify the parched earth.

Hand in hand with the struggle to overcome unfriendly nature went a fight to overcome the worn-out traditions of man. At that time the law of the United States declared that the water belonged to the man who owned the bank of the river. Now you cannot build an irrigation system so long as the water in the river is owned by the man who owns its bank. There had to be some sort of law whereby water could be taken from the river and legally spread over the land. The first men who dug irrigation ditches out in Colorado were sent to jail. It became necessary deliberately to violate the man-made law and accept punishment for the violation in order to convince a Supreme Court judge that the public welfare demanded a new law. After a number of men had gone to jail for trying to do a perfectly reasonable thing, three Supreme Court judges discovered why it was legal to take the water out of the river without consulting the owner of the bank.

But this victory did not end the struggle. Next came a fight against the contemporary economic world. The corporations came in and forced down the price of the land's products. The great power companies came in and tried to capture the natural power in the rivers and mountains for themselves. It was a battle on all fronts. Yet in the end the Great American Desert blossomed as the rose. The original pioneers died in poverty but later generations reaped the benefit of their prophetic vision.

Years later there arose other conquerors very similar in temperament and disposition to those who defeated the desert. Souls like Jane Addams, Graham Taylor and Robert A. Woods became the prophets who saw the Holy City in the midst of urban chaos. Up to 1890 American religious and social idealism played around the frontiers of a rapidly developing continent. The eyes of the conquerors of waste places sought a new society on the new land. By 1890, however, all the new land was occupied. Opportunities were no longer to be found in farming, mining or forestry. The so-called extractive industries had reached the saturation point. Opportunities were now to be found in factories and the accompanying vocations which make up what men do in cities. The new populations were beginning to concentrate in a strip of territory about two hundred miles wide stretching from the Mississippi river to the Atlantic coast, along the base of the Great Lakes and the Erie canal. This was a new migration. Hitherto northern Europe had been the great contributor of peoples. Now Italians, Poles, Czechs, Jews and other peoples from southern Europe, with strange customs and stranger languages, crowded into the cities which were owned and ruled by old-line Americans. As they saw their cities rapidly filling with these aliens many Americans were overwhelmed by a sense of despair. Here was a threat to the culture they were laboring to establish, an innocent but insidious attack upon the American way of life. Their only hope lay in strenuous conversion of these people to the so-called American way. It was a time of great anxiety. Social enthusiasm had to be turned from the western frontier to the places where great masses of men lived together.

So far as the religious forces and many forces which did not profess religion were concerned, Graham Taylor, Jane Addams and Robert A. Woods became important leaders in this transition. Theirs was a pilgrimage of the holy imagination. They moved into the center of the teeming urban populations and in a great act of self-identification took the city's problems on themselves. To them the newcomers were not objects of horror, but people to be understood. They followed the path of John Woolman. They believed that these people loved their children and were

ambitious for their advancement, that they suffered when
their children and neighbors suffered, that injustice and
bad politics were to be measured by their effect in the lives
of ordinary men. They sought to understand and, having
understood, formulated their understanding for a reluc-
tant world.

A few years later, out of this group of prophets, another
group arose. Strife and conflict were rife in some of the
great industries. In Chicago, for instance, the clothing
workers suffered under a sweatshop system which, while it
produced cheap clothes, left the workers without an opportunity to satisfy their legitimate needs and desires. A
small group of men of which James Mullenbach and Sid-
ney Hillman were important members were convinced
that it was possible to build an industrial society wherein
men should work as economic citizens rather than as wage
slaves. For many years they struggled, believing always
that justice and fair dealing could win out over a world
that was held together only by force and fear. Theirs was
a new desert to be conquered for civilization.

〜〜

There is a Christian word by which we describe the qualities of men who venture out beyond the boundaries of custom and become contenders for a redeeming God. That
word is " love." But love has been so softened by sentimentality that it has lost some of its power to challenge
men. It is, however, the best word we have. What is this
love?

Love is divine ecstasy. Margaret Montague, facing the
fact that she must become increasingly deaf and blind, enters into an experience whereby she can say she is madly

in love with every human being and every living creature. Love is that. Love is psychic power. Stanley Daly, a hardened criminal, discovers that love releases more power in his life than was ever released by hate and he writes a book entitled *Love Can Open Prison Doors*. Love is that. Love is capacity for identification with the most needy of God's creatures. John Woolman lives by putting himself in the place of the Negro and the Indian and the disinherited. Love is that. Love seeks the spiritual maturity of those with whom the lover comes in contact. Love is fidelity to something more than inclination in the relationship of husband and wife, parent and child. It is that which redeems the relationship of the sexes.

Love is neighborliness. It is that continuing attitude in the face-to-face contacts of the neighborhood which makes people feel a sense of lonesomeness when the good neighbor has gone. Love is public-mindedness. It is Governor Altgeld, with political reputation secure, laying that reputation upon the altar of justice by pardoning men of whose innocence he is satisfied and taking upon himself the hatred of a respectable world. It is Zola, candidate for the highest honors of France, sacrificing them all in the interests of justice to a member of a hated race. It is Graham Taylor thinking and working for Chicago in his last conscious hour. Love is the capacity to seek justice in controversies which are weighted heavily by motives of class-conscious antipathy.

Love is what Paul said it was — capacity to be patient, to seek no evil; love is not envious or boastful, it does not put on airs, it is not rude, it does not insist on its rights, it does not become angry, it is not resentful, it is not happy over injustice, it is happy only with the truth. Love will bear anything, believe anything, hope for anything, endure anything. Love will never die out. If there is inspired preaching it will pass away, if there is ecstatic speaking it will cease, if there is knowledge it will pass away. So faith, hope and love endure, and the greatest of these is love.

John Woolman and Graham Taylor and all the desert conquerors represent the doctrine of divine love breaking forth in social projects. To be sure, they had no clear-cut programs but they had that from which programs must stem. They had social passion; they had a concern; they had the will to be benevolent. They had what I call the holy imagination — that is, imagination that envelops people with compassion, with a sense of oneness, with humanity. That attitude, to my mind, is basic to any kind of social program.

The holy imagination is something that roots in the ecstasy of divine love. If social conflict and social need are to be dealt with, this passion must be kept alive. It is the function of the church to keep it alive. If the church fails in this function the flame will flicker out, and then all programs of social adjustment will become legalistic garments which can be fitted to humanity for a while; but humanity will ultimately throw them off because the designers did not first of all study in the school of compassion the inward nature of man.

These prophetic groups are now faced with one of the greatest struggles in human history, a struggle not unlike that in the early Roman Empire, when the little in-group in western Palestine contended with Caesar. Today also totalitarian states claim ultimate sanctity for themselves and their short-time objectives. They spit upon compassion and declare that hatred is the dynamic of society.

They force men into their image instead of allowing them to grow into the image of God. They remove from the individual all responsibility save that of blind obedience.

A sense of responsibility on the part of the individual is the very cornerstone of the democratic structure. But it should be emphasized that man's sense of responsibility is not built by his focusing on himself. There is a sense in which he must focus on himself.

> To thine own self be true,
> And it must follow, as the night the day,
> Thou canst not then be false to any man.

If a man fails to do what is right as he sees it he cannot be true to any larger issue. But man's belief in himself alone cannot sustain him. When Admiral Byrd passed a winter in a dugout on an Antarctic ice barrier only twenty degrees from the South Pole, he nearly perished by asphyxiation from the fumes of his gasoline engine and his oil-burning stove. But even in his terrible weakness he felt that to give up would be betrayal. At the basis of his belief that he must hold out lay a conviction that a power beyond himself was on his side and was demanding his allegiance. " I am not alone; there is a power — many call it God." [2] So man's sense of responsibility roots in the conviction that he is not alone. He is not alone because what he is he owes partly to his neighbor. He is not alone because he finds himself in discovering, defining and defending great causes. He is working with God.

Particularly when he makes decisions as to his loyalties man must remember God. Operating in these areas there is always an abundance of apostles who attempt to organize the wills of men around their own idea of what is su-

premely worth while. Some appeal to this practical absolute and some to that — to race or class prejudice, to special privilege, to self-will. Here is the first crisis in ethical
conduct. It has to do with the conflict of self-will over
the will for the universal and all-inclusive good as conceived by the person. The second conflict, which grows
out of the first and is even more acute, has to do with how
that good is discovered. It is just at this point that the demand for selflessness is likely to land the individual in
bondage to the past, to custom and law, and to add a religious sanction to the *status quo*. A totalitarian state or
a totalitarian industry can easily ask its members to be
loyal and give up their self-will. If, however, the people
relinquish their own self-will to a will which is defined by
the self-will of someone else, or is just the self-will of a
larger group, the inevitable result is some kind of slavery.

If Hitler is right when he says that the mass of the people
are " silly sheep," there is no hope for democracy. For democracy presupposes that its individual members are capable of acting in responsible fashion.

The individual, then, is one focus of responsible living.
What he thinks of himself will play a role in his behavior.
But equally important are his relations to society and to
God. What society thinks of him and what God thinks of
him, together with his idea of himself, will determine his
behavior. Responsible living focuses in these three: the
individual, society and God. Hence the resources of responsibility must be looked for in all three directions. Let
us illustrate what we mean by responsible living.

When Governor Altgeld faced the question of pardoning those who he thought had been unjustly convicted in the Haymarket Riots he gave the matter careful consideration and finally concluded:

First — That the jury which tried the case was a packed jury selected to convict.

Second — That, according to the law as laid down by the Supreme Court, both prior to and again since the trial of this case, the jurors, according to their own answers, were not competent jurors, and the trial was, therefore, not a legal trial.

Third — That the defendants were not proven to be guilty of the crime charged in the indictment.

Fourth — That as to the defendant Neebe, the state's attorney had declared at the close of the evidence that there was no case against him, and yet he had been kept in prison all these years.

Fifth — That the trial judge was either so prejudiced against the defendants, or else so determined to win the applause of a certain class in the community, that he could not and did not grant a fair trial.[3]

One morning the governor announced to " Buck " Hinrichsen:

" I am going to pardon Fielden, Schwab and Neebe this morning. I thought you might like to sign the papers in person rather than have your signature affixed by your chief clerk." He looked at Hinrichsen " rather curiously."

" Do you think it good policy to pardon them? " asked Hinrichsen. Before Altgeld could answer, Hinrichsen quickly added that he did not think it was.

Altgeld struck his desk with his fist.

" It is right! " [4]

The raging of the respectable people of the United States knew no bounds. Young Theodore Roosevelt was espe-

cially vociferous in his denunciation. Willis J. Abbot offered to introduce Roosevelt to Altgeld.

. . . Roosevelt reared up and in a strident voice, heard
through the Pullman car in which they were riding, announced
he would not meet Altgeld socially — " Because, sir, I may at
any time be called upon to meet the man sword to sword upon
the field of battle. . . . The sentiment now animating a large
proportion of our people can only be suppressed, as the Com-
mune in Paris was suppressed, by taking ten or a dozen of their
leaders out, standing . . . them against a wall, and shooting
them dead. I believe it will come to that." [5]

Today we are witnessing a strange realignment of public opinion with reference to the relative merits of Theodore Roosevelt and John Peter Altgeld.

In thus setting himself against the prejudices of a whole
nation and acting in accordance with his sense of justice,
Altgeld demonstrated responsible living. Responsible living includes the courage and capacity to break with all en-
vironmental securities and to outline adventurous programs of new good. There are those who warn us that men
may become too responsible for their society and so wax
conceited through success or land in despair through failure. These sages fail to recognize that the really difficult
task is to secure men who will not dodge responsibility.
Human beings easily take refuge in bluffing, delusion, cyn-
icism and suspicion. They make a cult of self-defense or
take refuge in false reports and hearsay. Few will face the
situation honestly and with humble intellectual alertness.
This is still the narrow road which will not entice the many
who travel the easy highroad of irresponsibility. The first
task in securing responsible human beings is to strip the
irresponsible of their alibis.

These alibis are of three main varieties. The individual absolves himself of obligation and blames social conditions, or the mass of men, or God, for the state of affairs. Let us consider first those alibis whereby the individual transfers his responsibility to God. The Puritan in the United States thirsted after responsibility as the hart panteth after the water brooks. His theology, heavily loaded with the doctrine of predestination, working back of his moral determination to govern himself, gave him something of a messianic trend of mind. It was his passion for self-government, however, and not his predestinarian theology which made him responsible. Men of weaker fiber found it easy to interpret the doctrine of predestination in a way that relieved them of all responsibility. Thus a certain Chicago minister opposed revivals on the ground that a certain number of men were going to be saved whatever they did or failed to do, and the rest would be lost anyway; so why bother? In my boyhood the minister of our Presbyterian church always discounted the public-mindedness of the Unitarian editor of our local paper, a Mr. Hayward. " Old Hayward," he used to say, " has to be good; he doesn't believe in Christ." Some time ago a notable sermon was preached from a Chicago pulpit on the general theme of civic reform. There were three kinds of cities, the pastor said. One was the City of Lust, the predatory city in which the ruling forces extorted riches from a suffering public. The second was the City of Rational Reform, struggling to bring in by human effort a regime in which human welfare would be paramount — a city of good homes, good streets, parks and civic centers. But its future, the pastor said, seemed very problematical; and even should it be attained it would be a City of Pride. He then directed our thought to a third city, the Holy City which Jehovah would some day hang upon our municipal Christmas tree if we would wait in faith. The audience voted for the third city since no effort seemed necessary for its realization.

The second class of alibis, by which the individual transfers his responsibility to the mass of men, commonly takes the form of " Everybody's doing it." This is the formula by which the tax dodger salves his conscience, by which the average citizen builds up his faith in major pressure groups. If enough people can be organized in pressure groups to attain our desires we are quite certain that our desires are right. " It is good policy " is another form of the same alibi. " Everybody " believes in reliance upon force, justifies the building of larger and better battleships. Thus we hand over to the mob obligations which belong to the individual.

Then there is the alibi of claiming special privilege. We drive down the street asserting that we have a friend at court and so can disregard the traffic light. Our father is a political big shot. We are a member of such and such a club and carry a certain kind of insurance. We belong to this preferred class or that chosen people. So we need not obey the regulations; those are for common men. We remove ourselves from the realm of moral obligation. We transfer our responsibility to those who allow us to be a member of the privileged class.

Superficial interpretation of the findings of science provides a specious alibi. We stretch the theory of economic determinism to cover all of life, and assert that climate or soil or some cosmic accident is responsible for all the ills of mankind. Some time ago I read a brochure which argued that the sense of responsibility depends entirely on the quality and amount of sunlight. Too much sunlight accompanied by a high altitude, the writer said, generates irresponsibility, and he cited the bad behavior of Colorado high school children as proof. This kind of half-truth is made to order for the seeker of alibis. Again, scientists maintain that man is to a great degree the product of the combination of topography, sunlight and rainfall which determine the yield of agriculture and hence have a bearing on birth and death rates, health and longevity. Certain of the scientists point to drouth, flood and desert as physical determinants by which man can be overwhelmed. However, even the desert can be transformed by irrigation canals and frost can be fought with smudge pots. Anyone who looks at a map of the United States of a hundred years ago sees large areas called the " Great American Desert." What has become of that desert? Both the Malthusian doctrine and the doctrine of economic determinism must be severely modified in view of man's ability to modify nature.

Another type of alibi is the affirmation of a petty moral conviction with such vehemence that it completely occupies the moral horizon and leaves no room for a sense of responsibility in other spheres. We lay the burdens we ought to carry on the dead shoulders of our ancestors. We say that the old virtues are good enough for us and we refuse to investigate their applicability to new situations. Or we magnify a minor virtue and exalt petty examples. An evangelist recently praised Dillinger because he did not smoke or drink. That preacher obscured for his audience the fact that Dillinger robbed and murdered all over the Mississippi valley. Those commit the same sin who are so dazzled by the virtues of hard work, frugality and thrift that they fail to see that large sections of our population live by owning and others do not have a chance to work or save. Not wholly unrelated to these is the man who asserts that because he is smart enough to do so he is at liberty to play tricks on the public. *Caveat emptor*, " Let the buyer beware," has long been the trader's motto. The great lawyer or banker who outwits the law by violating its spirit and declares that the public can have no complaint if he makes use of the cleverness nature has given him, has a conscience no better than the trader's.

Now it is a fact that the nature of the social order has a bearing on the character of its members. It may encourage individuals to take responsibility or discourage them from doing so. The sense of responsibility grows by exercise. Opportunity to be responsible will, over a term of years, affect our capacity to be responsible, and lack of such opportunity will cause that capacity to shrivel up. What kind of order we belong to is in the first place a matter of accident. But whatever the nature of that order, we must not use it to manufacture alibis for our failure to act responsibly. We excuse our neglect to protest against abuses by saying that censorship hinders freedom of speech. We discover that we cannot market a good product because there is no demand for it, that we cannot pay good wages because the general wage-level will not permit us to do so. There is a degree of truth in all these alibis. But in the main they only obscure our obligation to create a society in which we can manifest good behavior. In other words, we are responsible for creating a social order in which we can be responsible.

The conviction that we must create such an order is the first step in creating responsible people. The second is to open up to the individual the legitimate resources of responsible living; that is, a belief that the order of the universe is such that it demands responsible living and moral decision; that this basic order provides a standard for human conduct; and that human behavior can be organized through human agencies.

Let me illustrate this statement in terms of the life of Cecil Rhodes. William T. Stead thus expounds Rhodes' philosophy of life. The statement appeals to our sense of humor, but it illustrates our point:

Rhodes began by assuming that there was a fifty per cent chance a God existed. Take it a God did exist. What would this God want of man?

It was a question Rhodes was prepared to answer. God would want man not only to look like him, but to act like him. Man, therefore, had to find out what God was doing, and do the same.

What was God doing? Darwin had said it. God was perfecting the race through natural selection and the weeding out of the unfit. It remained merely for man to follow this lead and God's will was done.

The eyes of Rhodes were after God. He looked to see what, in this process of selection and elimination, God had achieved. Which, among all the people, had he brought to flower?

With all modesty, Rhodes could not help admitting that it was the English-speaking peoples that followed the highest ideal of justice, liberty and peace: the people of Great Britain, her dominions, and America.

The conclusion was clear. If Rhodes wished to please and follow God, he had, in whatever way he could, to promote the unity and extend the influence of the English-speaking race. To himself, personally, he allotted the task of Africa.[6]

In 1877, spending the long vacation in Kimberley, Rhodes composed a document which, many years later, he sent to Stead:

" It often strikes a man," says the document, grappling still, in the worrying Rhodes way, with his Ruskin-Darwin-Aristotle theme, " to inquire what is the chief good in life. To one the thought comes that it is a happy marriage, to another great wealth, to a third travel, and so on, and as each seizes the idea, he more or less works for its attainment for the rest of his existence. To myself, thinking over the same question, the wish came to make myself useful to my country. . . . I contend that we are the first race in the world, and that the more of the world we inhabit, the better it is for the human race. I contend that every acre added to our territory provides for the birth of more of the English race, who otherwise would not be brought into existence. Added to which the absorption of the greater portion of the world under our rule simply means the end of all wars."

And here and now he decides that he will work " for the furtherance of the British empire, for the bringing of the whole civilized world under British rule, for the recovery of the United States, for the making of the Anglo-Saxon race into one empire. What a dream! But yet it is probable! It is possible! " [7]

Now analysis of this statement reveals that it contains a belief as to what God is doing in history: God is working for the survival of the fittest, and the agent through which he works is the British empire. This assumption issues in two further ideas: a philosophy of life and the choice of a vocation on the basis of which Rhodes criticizes his own behavior and that of others and plans a future outcome. Rhodes' notion that God is working for the survival of the fittest and calls upon the English race to populate as much of the world as possible is of course fantastic, but the perception on which it is founded is sound. Responsible living must be grounded in a philosophy of life which has also a cosmic and a social reference.

Man's resources for responsible living then can be classified under three heads. First are all those considerations which come out of his reading of the divine drama. If he believes that the nature of reality is such as to encourage him in the pilgrimage toward spiritual maturity he will work with confidence and assurance. Second is what man thinks of himself and what others think of him. We climb with others the ladder of responsible living. We seek spiritual maturity for others and we associate with those who encourage it in us. There is no greater delusion than the delusion of the self-made man. Man does not make himself. He shares with others a belief to which both can contribute and which makes them both.

The third resource for responsible living is the community which gives the individual opportunity to be responsible. Responsible living is in a real sense the product of the habitual taking of responsibility in situations which demand it. People who, for a long time, are denied the opportunity of making free choices in social conduct gradually lose the capacity to do so. Only as we are challenged by a social order which believes in freedom can we really become responsible.

NOTES

1 Fletcher Dobyns, *The Underworld of American Politics* (Los Angeles: Author, 1932), p. 211.

2 See Richard E. Byrd, *Alone* (New York: G. P. Putnam's Sons, 1938).

3 Henry Barnard, *Eagle Forgotten: The Life of John Peter Altgeld* (Indianapolis: Bobbs-Merrill Co., 1938), p. 217.

4 *Ibid.*, p. 214.

5 *Ibid.*, p. 386. (Roosevelt denied that he made this statement.)

6 Cited by Sarah Gertrude Millin, *Rhodes* (London: Chatto & Windus, 1936), p. 67.

7 *Ibid.*

How the American People Became Irresponsible

The coming of a democratic society awaits the coming of people who want to make choices, take responsibility and seek fellowship. You cannot have responsible people unless you are willing to create a society in which they can be responsible. On the whole, as things now stand democracy seems to be holding on to God and freedom and neglecting responsibility and common welfare, while totalitarian societies are holding on to responsibility and common welfare and neglecting God and freedom. The question is whether, while maintaining God and freedom — the religious values which are necessary to spiritual maturity — democracy can move on to a needed emphasis on responsibility and common welfare in a world-wide society.

The American social conscience began as a theocracy in a village. That theocracy gave us our first responsible living and that village our first concept of common welfare. In this theocratic experiment there are germ ideas which will be useful in our tumultuous modern search for new definitions of responsibility and new concepts of common welfare.

Puritanism offered to those early New England colonists participation in the final act of a drama of divine redemption. It profoundly believed that the appearance of Jesus Christ constituted the greatest event in human his-

tory.   Its ethics were biblical, and they were definite
enough to struggle for supremacy in a world of competing
ideas.   It founded in the western hemisphere a new commonwealth based on the Word of God and designed to save
men.   Puritanism believed in the organization of communities on what it conceived as a divinely revealed plan.
It believed that God was the redeemer of persons and
communities.   And this is the abiding essence of its religious social message.

In early American life, religion, neighborliness, and the
economic and political arrangements were coextensive in
their acknowledged spheres of influence and interpene-
trating in their relationship to one another.   At that time
there existed what I call responsible living or, if you will,
Christian public-mindedness.   Responsible living always
has this double rootage.   It roots in what men think of
themselves and their fellows, and it requires an appropriate constellation of vocations and communities through
which what they think of themselves can find expression.
A stable society is one in which there are people who want
what they ought to want, and also communities in which
the people who want what they ought to want can get what
they want.

Cotton Mather saw the New World commonwealth as a
part of the divine drama of the redemption of humanity.
Boston, the metropolis of that commonwealth, was necessarily important.   Mather held that God was a redeemer
of persons and of peoples (corporate communities) , and in
his famous address, " The History of Boston Related and
Improved," he based a whole code of civic-mindedness for
Boston on his doctrine of a redeeming God who was redeeming Boston as well as the persons who live in Boston.
Sin was disloyalty and righteousness was loyalty to that re-

deeming God. After reciting what God has done for Boston, Mather says:

And now will the *Justices* of the town set themselves to consider, How they may help to suppress all growing vices among us?

Will the *Constables* of the town set themselves to consider, How they may help to prevent all evil orders among us?

There are some who have the eye of the town so much upon them, that the very name of *Townsmen* is that by which they are distinguished. Sirs, will you also consider how to help the affairs of the town, so as that all things may go well among us?

Moreover, may not *School-Masters* do much to instill principles of religion and civility, as well as other points of good education, into the children of the town? Only let the town well encourage its well-deserving school-masters.

There are some officers; but concerning *all,* there are these two things to be desired: First, it is to be desired that such officers as are chosen among us, may be chosen in the fear of God. May none but pious and prudent men, and such as love the town, be chosen to serve it.

And, secondly, it is to be desired that officers of several sorts would often come together for consultation. Each of the sorts by themselves, may they often come together to consult. " What shall we do to serve the town in those interests which are committed unto our charge? "

Oh! what a deplorable thing will it be for persons entrusted with talents (your opportunities to serve the town are so many talents!) and they never seriously consider, " What good shall I do with my talents in the place where God hath stationed me? "

And will the representatives of the town be considered among the rest, as entrusted with some singular advantages for our help? The Lord give you understanding in all things!

God help the town to manifest all that Piety which a town so helped of him is obliged unto! [1]

The Puritan theocracy so carefully expounded by
Mather broke down. But the idea lived on in simple
churches, in schoolhouses and colleges, among preachers
and teachers who used the Bible and John Locke to prove
that a good state is good only when it exists for the well-
being of the people; that a good government is a covenant
between men and no government can remain good without the consent of the people; that there is a powerful good
God in whose name men have the right to defy all oppression; that there are a law of nature and a law of revelation
which give a point of reference from which to defy man-
made law.

Alexis de Tocqueville was neither preacher nor teacher,
but his sociological theory of responsible living, simply
and delightfully set forth in *Democracy in America*, follows the line laid out by the theocrats. In this volume,
which appeared a little over a hundred years ago — in
1835 to be exact — De Tocqueville says:

In the United States the sovereign authority is religious;
there is no country in the whole world in which the Christian
religion retains a greater influence over the souls of men than
in America; and there can be no greater proof of its utility, and
of its conformity to human nature, than that its influence is
most powerfully felt over the most enlightened and free nation
of the earth.

I have remarked that the members of the American clergy in
general, without even excepting those who do not admit religious liberty, are all in favor of civil freedom; but they do not
support any particular political system. They keep aloof from
parties and from public affairs. In the United States religion
exercises but little influence upon the laws and upon the details

of public opinion, but it *directs the manners* of the community, and by regulating domestic life it regulates the state.

I do not question that the great austerity of manners which is observable in the United States arises, in the first instance, from religious faith. Religion is often unable to restrain man from the numberless temptations of fortune; nor can it check that passion for gain which every incident of his life contributes to arouse, but its influence over the mind of woman is supreme, and women are the protectors of morals.[2]

Thus, as De Tocqueville sees it, responsible living roots first of all in a responsible person as the unit of a responsible society. This responsible individual he finds in the American pioneer who has temporarily taken up his residence in the wilderness. He is equipped with a Bible, an ax and a newspaper. He is acquainted with the past, curious about the future and ever ready to argue about the present.

The second unit of responsible living De Tocqueville finds in the American family:

There is certainly no country in the world where the tie of marriage is so much respected as in America, or where conjugal happiness is more highly or worthily appreciated. In Europe almost all the disturbances of society arise from the irregularities of domestic life. To despise the natural bonds and legitimate pleasures of home, is to contract a taste for excesses, a restlessness of heart, and the evil of fluctuating desires.

Agitated by the tumultuous passions which frequently disturb his dwelling, the European is galled by the obedience which the legislative powers of the state exact. But when the American retires from the turmoil of public life to the bosom of his family, he finds in it the image of order and of peace. There his pleasures are simple and natural, his joys are innocent and calm; and as he finds that an orderly life is the surest path to happiness, he accustoms himself without difficulty to moderate his opinions as well as his tastes.

Whilst the European endeavors to forget his domestic troubles by agitating society, the American derives from his own home that love of order which he afterwards carries with him into public affairs.[3]

De Tocqueville then speaks of the democratic ownership of property as the next safeguard of responsible living in the United States. This democratic ownership, he says, is insured by the law which provides that the big landed estates be divided equally among all the children at the time of the owner's death.

When the legislator has regulated the law of inheritance, he may rest from his labor. The machine once put in motion will go on for ages, and advance, as if self-guided, toward a given point. When framed in a particular manner, this law unites, draws together, and vests property and power in a few hands: its tendency is clearly aristocratic. On opposite principles its action is still more rapid; it divides, distributes, and disperses both property and power. Alarmed by the rapidity of its progress, those who despair of arresting its motion endeavor to obstruct it by difficulties and impediments; they vainly seek to counteract its effect by contrary efforts; but it gradually reduces or destroys every obstacle, until by its incessant activity the bulwarks of the influence of wealth are ground down to the fine and shifting sand which is the basis of democracy. When the law of inheritance permits, still more when it decrees, the equal division of a father's property among all his children, its effects are of two kinds: it is important to distinguish them from each other, although they tend to the same end.

In virtue of the law of partible inheritance, the death of every proprietor brings about a kind of revolution in property; not only do his possessions change hands, but their very nature is altered, since they are parcelled into shares, which become smaller and smaller at each division. This is the direct and, as it were, the physical effect of the law. It follows then, that in countries where equality of inheritance is established by law, property, and especially landed property, must have a tendency to perpetual diminution. The effects, however, of such legislation would only be perceptible after a lapse of time, if the law was abandoned to its own working; for supposing the family to consist of two children (and in a country peopled as France is the average number is not above three), these children, sharing among them the fortune of both parents, would not be poorer than their father or mother.[4]

The next citadel of democracy is the township:

Townships are to liberty what primary schools are to science; they bring it within the people's reach, they teach men how to use and how to enjoy it. A nation may establish a system of free government, but without the spirit of municipal institutions it cannot have the spirit of liberty.

The American attaches himself to his home as the mountaineer clings to his hills.

The native of New England is attached to his township because it is independent and free. His cooperation in its affairs insures his attachment to its interest; the well-being it affords him secures his affection; and its welfare is the aim of his ambition and of his future exertions; he takes a part in every occurrence in the place; he practices the art of government in the small sphere within his reach; he accustoms himself to those forms which can alone insure the steady progress of liberty, he imbibes their spirit, he acquires a taste for order, comprehends the union or the balance of powers and collects clear practical notions on the nature of his duties and the extent of his rights.[5]

In the early period of American democracy, then, responsible living rooted first in man's sublime picture of himself as a part of the divine plan of the universe, in his

religion which made him humble and socially responsible.
It rooted also in a set of mutually supporting, simple political and economic vocations which gave abundant opportunity for the exercise of the divine calling. Religion
trained men to want what they ought to want, and the social order gave them an opportunity for realizing those
wants. Men spoke easily of justice and discussed all the
virtues and vices as important phases of life. Ethics had
not yet become an outlawed mental discipline.

To put it more briefly still: if you had been a member
of one of those communities you, along with others, would
have carried on the simple activities involved in home production and neighborhood consumption. The lawyer, the
baker, the candlestick-maker, labored in an economy tempered by religion and neighborliness and a sense of civic
duty. The shoemaker took care not to make a bad pair
of shoes, because he expected to meet on the street the
next day the man who was wearing the shoes. The farmer
took pains not to sell too many rotten eggs, because he expected to see at church the next Sunday the man who
bought the eggs. The politically inclined citizen took
thought about the laws he favored, because he expected
to have his acts reviewed at the next town meeting. The
religion which controlled manners controlled the public
order also, because the spheres of manners, economy and
politics were practically coextensive.

The village grew up. The village post road became an
international highway. The age of homespun became the
age of high-powered production in factory and on farm.
The democratic economy of simple, useful labor became
an autocratically owned system of corporations financed
out of a highly centralized, privately owned economic or-

der. But the ethics neither of democracy nor of Christianity grew up; they were content to remain in the village stage.

Yet it would be unfair to say that the adherents of Christian democratic ethics did not attempt to deal with the new economic situation. In the period between 1840 and 1850 the Owenites, the Associationists and the New England Transcendentalists all faced bravely the question of the ethics and organization of property, as their forebears in the period between 1700 and 1800 had faced the question of the ethics and organization of the state. As a result of their labors they could point to the democratization of landholding, the increasing freedom for women and freedom for slaves. But the Civil War was too much for them. It focused the attention of the nation on one issue and obliterated all the others, at least temporarily. After the Civil War the Republican party, which had been organized as a free-soil party for the democratization of landholding and the winning of more privileges for labor, was captured by the great industrialists, who made it the instrument of increasing their power. The social idealism of a Channing, a Parker and a Horace Greeley was largely forgotten, both by the holders of power and by the people.

In tracing the failure of the ethics of Christianity and democracy to escape from the village stage, we must first of all record the disintegration of the dream of the divine redemptive drama. Let us admit that it had to disintegrate. The legalistic, Bible-centered, upper-class controlled world of Cotton Mather had to break up. When Benjamin Franklin organized his Hellfire Club, Cotton Mather's world of responsible living began to fall to pieces. When he wrote his *Road to Wealth* he documented the be-

ginning of American Babbitry. God, for Franklin, became a great aid to success but not the inspirer of humility.
From the standpoint of administration the separation of
church from government was necessary but it resulted in
making religion a private matter and interest in it more or
less optional. Not to be able to discuss questions of commerce and politics was a sign of weakness, but ethics and
religion were discussed as we might discuss the hobbies in-
dulged in by a few.

Science in the meantime came to the forefront as the important phase of culture. The scientist was answering the
question which men who were controlling continents
wanted to have answered. He taught the techniques necessary in getting on — how to beat your competitor, not
how to treat him. He implemented equally the predatory
and the pious. Colleges with great laboratories which
taught the skills of science supplanted colleges which
taught the values that could motivate the will. Moreover,
science brought with it an ethical theory which was very
dear to the man who worshiped the " God of Getting-on."
That theory was Mr. Darwin's doctrine of the survival of
the fittest.

Another blow to public-minded thinking and living
came with the abandonment of the township as a unit of
social and political life and the arrival of the large city.
East of the Hudson, America was settled community-end
first. West of the Hudson, except where the New England
tradition was strongest, the newcomer settled without regard to the community. The town meeting disappeared.
Gradually there developed the big city with its mass-

minded population dominated by the metropolitan newspaper and the urban politician. Urban political machinery was something to be captured by propaganda in the interest of power. No recession in American ethical standards ever equaled the shift from the town meeting, which purposed to modify and socialize the struggle for power, to the urban society whose political machinery is regarded as a tool to be captured by men who desire power.

Great cities are essentially alike in being, as a high authority has called them, aggregations of separate self-centered units with no common purpose. Chicago will serve as an example. Chicago, it has been said, does not know why it exists; it has no soul. Some of its perversions have been dramatic enough to attract world attention. Chicago was shocked when Al Capone offered to be a good gangster if he were allowed the exclusive rights in the South Side beer racket. It was shocked by the Insull crash. It was shocked to find that its treasurer was four hundred thousand dollars short in his accounts — which four hundred thousand dollars, he jovially reported, he had lent to various political friends for trifling purposes. It was more recently shocked when the county assessor revealed that the wealthier citizens had annually hidden almost five hundred million dollars' worth of their personal property from the eyes of the collector of the personal property tax. It is now shocked by the fact that it has a blighted area covering at least forty square miles, the accumulated uncollectible tax deficit of which amounts to three hundred million dollars.

Nothing, however, could be further from true insight into the real nature of Chicago's perversions than to attribute them to personal failings on the part of individuals.

No more futile attitude could be imagined than that which assumes that the people of Chicago could make great moral progress by eliminating a few much dramatized individuals. The perversion is moral, but it is also organic, and to a large extent it is shared by all the citizens. A new standard of success has had right of way in this modern city. The best business has been that which made the most money. As Mr. Insull declared, his business was to make money. Wanting to make money, Mr. Insull had to have certain kinds of help — for instance, lawyers. His lawyers came from a profession which held aloft high standards of public-mindedness. Few people would contend that lawyers such as these, who have helped big business achieve its objectives, have been true to their own vocational standard. The perversion of business by the profit motive has dragged down with it the great profession of the law. Lawyers are employed by great corporations to help the corporation achieve its purposes.

The perversion of business carried with it also the perversion of the press. The State street merchants and the La Salle street bankers wield a mighty influence over the policies of the metropolitan papers. Pressure is consciously and unconsciously exercised. Many newspaper men have high standards but the newspapers of the metropolitan area reflect the metropolitan point of view. A young representative of the Associated Press recently drew up the following indictment:

The press is inaccurate; it misquotes persons interviewed; it deliberately fakes, makes improper sacrifices to speed and is oblivious to significant news in more remote fields.

Much truth to which the public is entitled is suppressed; news is distorted and colored with editorial opinion; by selection and emphasis it is made to conform to the newspaper's bias.

Commercialism has dulled the newspaper's interest in higher things; "impersonal" journalism lacks courage; the institutional press is bound by capitalistic sympathies.

The press is unfairly partisan in politics and in other matters; it maintains a "blacklist," and worships certain "sacred cows" (favored corporations).

Some newspapers invade privacy; they are textbooks of crime; scandal and sex stories are printed solely to sell the papers.

The atmosphere of a newspaper office is tainted by duplicity; they print what they do not believe.

The newspaper employs anonymity to evade personal responsibility; it does not perform its duties as a common carrier of information; good journalism protects bad journalism.

The newspaper is suspicious of anything new in government and hidebound in its conservatism.

Sensationalism distorts the news in most papers; the significance of news is less regarded than its human interest.

The real interest in the press is money-grabbing; its advocacy of improvements is limited to those favored by commercial interests.[6]

Along with this perversion of the press goes inevitably the perversion of politics. Business men say that business is for the sake of business. The politician naturally declares that politics is for the sake of the politician. "Bob Sweitzer was the best vote-getter in the Democratic party." So says the evening paper in writing the story of the county treasurer who came up with the four hundred thousand dollar shortage previously mentioned. But what does vote-getting in Chicago mean? To a great extent it means ability to pander to the selfish prejudices of the largest group of specialized interests. These interests may be and often are just the people in the ordinary precinct and ward who want employment. They may be the interests of racial groups who hunt in racial packs for city advantages. They may be the big public utilities. Being a vote-getter means being able to offer to these various groups of privilege-seekers some kind of selfish advantage which will cause them to deliver their votes on election day.

It has recently been said that all election policies are determined by people whose votes are bought and paid for by some kind of concession which requires of those who take part in the deal absolute blindness to considerations of public-mindedness. Mr. Insull, desiring to achieve his purposes as head of the " Insull empire," not only made enormous contributions to the campaign funds of Chicago and Illinois politicians, but granted special opportunities in his stock deals to the city's political bosses. His perversion was not essentially different from that of the ward-heeler who appeals to his friends to vote for a certain politician because the politician, if elected, will provide jobs for them.

With corrupt politics has come the gang. Our chief authority on racketeering has this to say about gangs and gangsters:

Five distinct but interdependent elements comprise the structure of any racket. These are: (1) business men; (2) leaders of organized labor; (3) politicians; (4) criminals; (5) lawyers.

Racketeering, in short, is a combination of business, labor unionism, politics, lawyers and the criminal underworld, the purpose of which is exploitation of commerce and the public through circumscribing the right to work and do business.

Accepting this as the definition of racketeering let us examine each unit of the racket structure and see what each hopes to derive from participation in it.

The business man seeks to create for himself and a favored few a monopoly in his particular field of service or trade, embarrassing his competitors, maintaining an arbitrary price for his commodity or service, even seeking to dictate enactment and application of laws that govern his business.

The leader of organized labor who betrays his trust and lends himself to a racket seeks first a monopoly of control over the workmen engaged in a given trade. This enables him to keep his treasury more full and to manipulate his main forces to the advantage of his co-conspirators and to the disadvantage of business men who dare to assert independence of the racket.

The politician by paralyzing the hand of the law is, of course, looking to campaign contributors, organization work and votes at election time and frequently also to participation in the profits of the conspiracy.

The criminal underworld finds lucrative employment to bomb, to commit arson, to slug, maim and kill, to terrorize an entire community into staying away from the polls at election time, and to fraudulent voting and terroristic practices at the polls, and latterly to control racketeering in its entirety.

The lawyer guides and protects the racketeers in the matter of counsel, before the courts, in the realm of politics, and often he is to be found exercising the powers of an actual officer of the racket union or association. It is true that he is paid large fees or salaries for his services but he is or should be grounded in a tradition of ethical conduct stretching the length of the recorded memory of man. Yet we find a certain type of lawyer the most important cog in the machinery of crime. He has twisted and distorted the law to suit the purposes of a criminal clientele, subverting the dignity of habeas corpus, making the " continuance " in criminal trials anathema to complainants and a solace to criminals, devising the clever legal instruments that constitute the charters of rackets, in this way providing

a respectable façade to fool the public. Any facilities of the
legal profession of discipline for such members seem to have
atrophied long ago.[7]

Along with the perversion of these major elements in
society goes the perversion of the schools. In a democratic
country, school funds are likely to be large and administrative positions lucrative. Our chief authority on education
thus describes the situation in the Chicago school system:

> With the exception of a few short intervals, the board of edu-
> cation of this city has been for at least twenty-five years the tool
> of the dominant political party. City Hall influence ordinarily
> has not invaded the educational branch of the system but has
> frequently invaded the business affairs for the purpose of
> spoils.[8]

The churches have not escaped the general corruption.
It would be nice to be able to say that the churches exist
as oases in a desert of public evil; it is not true. Churches
drift with the various social groups which maintain them.
They live in the midst of these social groups, they stabilize
them, but it is the rare church which can rise above the
ethics of self-preservation to some kind of public-mindedness which thinks in terms of the larger welfare.

This perversion of the functions of the city is but an
aspect of the larger perversion which misconceives the
function of the city with reference to the rest of the nation.
The city has frequently been looked upon as a social ultimate which operates entirely under laws of its own genius,
without regard to the rest of society. But what is a city?
It is the place where certain functions of national life

come together in great aggregations. The city is just one-third of the national process. It is the place where the money-lender, the manufacturer, the trader and the professional man exist side by side, not for themselves but manifestly in order to play a part in a national process, two-thirds of which is outside the city. When towns were simple, it was easy to say and believe that the town ought to be a service center to the surrounding country, but in the great mass organization of the modern city this original functional relationship is entirely obscured. The city as a whole is terribly and exclusively interested in its own growth and development. It asks no ultimate questions about its relationship to all those national functions which exist outside it.

I do not believe that the average city man harbors antipathies toward his rural compatriots. Some, like Mencken, may use nasty words and refer to the farmer as a yokel and a peasant. Some have forgotten that agriculture exists and are irritated when reminded of the fact. But the average city man merely builds an impenetrable wall about himself by attributing to himself urban-mindedness. Nobody knows what urban-mindedness is, but whatever it is the urban man thinks he has it and behind it he hides and hopes to defy analysis. But let us see whether this urban-mindedness — or urbanization — is not susceptible to being reduced to its essential elements. What do I mean when I use the term " urbanization "?

Urbanization is the way in which that part of our population who live in cities think and act in their capacity as lenders of money. They want what they call " sound money," which means that debt-paying is an unqualified obligation.

Urbanization is the way in which that part of our population who live in cities think and act in their capacities as buyers of raw material for manufacture and sellers of manufactured products. They want protective tariffs for themselves but urge the farmer never to adopt a political remedy for an economic disease.

Urbanization is the way in which that part of our population who live in cities act in their capacity as wage earners. They fight inflation, which lowers the buying power of their dollar, and they fight a rise in the price of food. Urbanization, in brief, is a wild growth in the body social. If it is not checked it will kill the body.

∿∿

ˋ The spiritual heir of the Christian democrats who founded this nation faces a dilemma. The modern Christian has a Christian conscience which believes in love and mutual aid. His ethic is sound. He clings, in theory, to the ideas of responsibility and common welfare. But he is unable to act upon that ethic, for he has developed moral energy for organizing only a small phase of life. Modern political and economic energy, however, equipped with science, has given him a world which extends beyond the borders of his city and of his nation, and is organized on the theory of the survival of the fittest.

When the theocracy of the days of homespun and the village began to fail several alternative paths were opened up. One group took the road of evangelism and began to explore the inner recesses of the heart. Presently they found themselves on the path of otherworldliness and began to dynamite the social order with the doctrine of the second coming of Christ. This doctrine shot religion into the sky. In its social expression it built orphanages and houses of refuge.

Another group followed the rationalists. They allied the doctrines of human rights and of the divine right of property and became the fathers of American Babbitry. God, for them, became a great help in the acquiring of wealth. This doctrine shot religion into the ground. In its social expression it displayed enthusiasm for those institutions which helped the individual make good in his own name.

A third road was laid out by William E. Channing, Theodore Parker and Horace Bushnell, who sought to reconstitute the American dream in terms of a social order which had railroad trains and factories but retained the spirit of the community and its sense of personal relationship. They wanted to keep religion on earth and make science its servant, not its master.

But the road of Channing, Parker and Bushnell has proved to be harder to build and the jungle into which it led far more impenetrable than was at first suspected. It is not just the jungle of the modern city; it is the jungle of a whole civilization built around the principles of survival of the fittest and the struggle for power. There are those who think that that road cannot be built and they are turning back to the first way. They are content with a religion which deals with the crises of the inner life and in various ways are trying to find relief in some form of divine intervention. That solution, of course, does not affect society as a whole. The second road, that of the individualists, is choked by the debris of war and financial debacle.

We must turn back to the third road. Slow as is the process, that road must be built. Man has the right to rely on

God for help but God does not relieve man of the necessity of building the road. We must recapture our sense of a constant written into the cosmic structure which has significance for what we think of ourselves and of our fellows.

But while recovering this awareness of meaning, we must not neglect that other rootage of public-mindedness, the appropriate constellation of vocations and communities in which what we think of ourselves and our fellows can find appropriate and satisfying expression. We must create the democratic community in which we can be responsible, and we must extend that sense of community into the public relationships of life.

NOTES

1 Cotton Mather, "The History of Boston Related and Improved," *Old South Leaflets* (gen. ser., Boston, 1896), I, 97.

2 Alexis de Tocqueville, *Democracy in America* (New York: Colonial Press, 1899), pp. 308–9.

3 *Ibid.,* p. 309.

4 *Ibid.,* pp. 35–36.

5 *Ibid.*

6 From a report by a student in one of the author's classes.

7 H. B. Hostetter, "The Rising Tide of Racketeering," an address delivered before a "Rethinking Chicago" meeting and incorporated into *Rethinking Chicago* (a mimeographed document in the Department of Social Ethics, Chicago Theological Seminary), p. 55.

8 Charles H. Judd, "How Are the Children of Chicago to be Educated?" *Rethinking Chicago,* p. 88.

Democracy's Competitors

Democracy makes certain philosophic assumptions, on which it bases its political theory and its attitude toward religion. In a recent article in the *Political Science Quarterly* Professor Charles E. Merriam of the University of Chicago defines these assumptions as: (1) The essential dignity of all men and the importance of protecting and cultivating personality primarily on a fraternal rather than on a differential basis; (2) a constant trend in human affairs toward the perfectibility of mankind; (3) the fact that the gains of commonwealths are essentially mass gains and should be diffused through the mass by whom they were created as rapidly and as fairly as possible; (4) the desirability of popular control in the last analysis over basic questions of policy and direction with recognized procedures for the formulation of such policies and their execution; (5) confidence in the possibility of conscious social change accomplished by consent rather than by violence.[1]

In relation to religion democracy has been closely associated with Protestantism. It has demonstrated a religious respect for the individual and has maintained freedom of worship. It has left the church free to discover and determine that which is worthy of supreme devotion. It thinks of church, school and state as exercising a fellowship of functions, but concedes to none of them an exclusive right to organize the human will. In matters of social change democracy believes in supremacy of truth, education, popular vote and parliamentary action. As between its various agencies, such as religion, education, industry and government, democracy insists on separation, freedom and unity through cooperation.

To sum up, democracy is characterized by an emphasis on the importance of the individual and of the various functional groups. Unity comes not at the beginning of the process but at the end, through cooperation. Social change must be brought about through persuasion, not by force. Though it stresses the importance of a shared welfare, democracy has not hesitated to allow freedom of initiative despite the fact that this has involved a high degree of competition; it believes in keeping society open at the bottom and at the top. Democracy is that kind of society which, in its assumptions, structure and habits, hopes to leave people when it is through with them more mature ethically and spiritually than when it found them.

Thus the ultimate basis of democracy is moral. The cries of despair that rise from within the democratic ranks focus attention on the moral ideals which lie at the root of the system.

Democracy's competitors are at the door. They have been able to advance so far because they have taken up two of democracy's forgotten words — responsibility and common welfare. To be sure these competitors renounce God, they ignore the fact that there can be no real responsibility without freedom, and they are infatuated with the idea of the state. Nevertheless, the fact remains that they have at least attempted to solve the problem of an organic society.

Those of us who live in an unchallenged democracy find

it difficult to understand the system of which we are a part. A young student once remarked: " Understanding democracy for an American is like a bee making honey; it sticks to his legs and he can't see it." But by looking carefully at democracy's great present competitors we may arrive, through contrast, at a better understanding of our own system.

Every system, whether it be fascism or communism, democracy or feudalism, is characterized by certain persistent factors on the basis of which it can be analyzed and understood. We can ask of each system certain great questions through which, as through windows, we can examine its qualities. These are the questions:

1. Around what values does this system organize?

2. Where are the originating sources of these values?

3. What are the ways of social change advocated by this system?

4. What social and economic arrangement between the major functions — religion, education, industry and state — is provided?

5. What basic religious ideas are held and how are these ideas provided for in religious institutions?

Let us focus attention on democracy, represented by the United States, democratic collectivism by Denmark and Scandinavia, fascism by Italy, national socialism by Germany, and communism by Russia, and ask each our questions.

If we ask, What are the basic values? the answers are:

Democracy: The individual, the right of private initiative, private judgment and private property.

Democratic Collectivism: The individual and the group.
National Socialism: The *Volk* and its racial welfare.
Fascism: The state and national supremacy.
Communism: The proletariat mass and the welfare of the proletariat.

If we ask, What are the originating sources of values? the answers are:

Democracy: Every man.
Democratic Collectivism: The individual and the group.
National Socialism: The race; the elite.
Fascism: The whole state speaking through the elite.
Communism: The proletariat mass.

If we ask, What are the ways of social change and social control advocated by the systems? the answers are:

Democracy: Supremacy of truth, education, popular vote and parliamentary action.
Democratic Collectivism: Freedom for truth and culture, co-operative collectivism; state action as product of parliamentary procedure.
National Socialism: Volk welfare supreme over truth; first emphasis on securing of power; rule through propaganda.
Fascism: Religious truth as a separate entity; power abides in state rule by state propaganda.
Communism: Power first, truth second; rule by power and propaganda.

If we ask, What are the ways of social arrangement between the major functions — religion, education, industry and government? the answers are:

Democracy: Laissez faire in theory, opportunity for the entrepreneur, actual special privilege for the money-lender, trader and manufacturer.

Democratic Collectivism: Large growth of cooperative movement; much of private industry still remains; state enters business at point where private industry is least adequate.

National Socialism: National planning through economic dictatorship; responsible leadership of entrepreneur; much government ownership; agricultural and middle classes privileged.

Fascism: National planning through dictatorship; state control of capitalist system; most business privately owned.

Communism: Abolition of capitalist system, state ownership of means of production and distribution; control largely in interest of urban proletariat, middle class eliminated; agriculture regimented.

If we ask, What are the basic religious ideas? the answers are:

Democracy: Religious respect for individual; largely Protestant in faith; freedom of worship maintained.

Democratic Collectivism: Church still free to discover and determine that which is worthy of supreme devotion; church, school and state maintain a fellowship of functions.

National Socialism: Religion to revert to tribal stage, church to be regimented in interest of *Volk* and state; state assumes many functions of church.

Fascism: Church and state exist in separated and unrelated functions.

Communism: Religion identified as instrument of slavery; state takes over church function of determining that which is worthy of supreme devotion; church abolished.

The contrast which these systems afford is overwhelming in its significance. The ethical issues threaten to create a new epoch. For three hundred years responsibility has been placed on the individual. Now, in a large part of world society, responsibility is not on the individual but on the group. Here is a fundamental shift. But such shifts in social ideas and methods have their source in some need, else they could not be maintained for more than a very short time. The opponents of democracy have something to say for themselves.

Draw a line between the Scandinavian countries on the west and Russia on the east, let it pass between Denmark and Germany, and follow down to the Mediterranean sea between France and Germany. On the west side of this line will lie most of the countries which have had experience with and still profess belief in the democratic method. On its east will be the countries which have undertaken the solution of social problems through resort to some kind of dictatorship. The line between the countries which are so distinguished will probably become sharper as the days go on.

If one were to approach intelligent citizens on the west side of this line and ask them their convictions about social methods, one would receive answers somewhat as follows:

We believe (they would say) that a democracy which trusts the people to cooperate in self-government is worth fighting for. We have no desire to be members of a totalitarian state.

We believe that education which respects individual judgment and does not turn a university into a group of " yes-men " is worth fighting for. We view with apprehension the shift of the center of educational control from standards which are indigenous to educational institutions to standards based on the short-time objectives of a racial group or of the state. The dictator who surrounds himself with educators who tell him what he wants to know will ultimately die of ignorance. We believe that our educational institutions render the best service to the common good in an environment which recognizes freedom of research and the right of private judgment. We will maintain a social order in which there is willingness to grant this freedom because we desire to have the service of free investigators rather than of intellectual slaves.

˅ We believe that a church which can stand over against the state and look the state in the face and criticize it in the name of the highest good is worth fighting for. Religious institutions are charged with the task of interpreting that which is worthy of supreme devotion. Freedom to do this without first making obeisance to any of the secondary values of race, class or nation, is an indispensable condition of social health.

We worship a God before whose will race, class and nation must walk humbly. This God is superior to every *Volk* God. The career of the God we worship is marked by successive triumphs over the false absolutes of empire and race. In early Christianity the battle against emperor worship was fought once and for all, and in early Judaism our God ceased to be the God of a preferred people. He cannot now be made to serve the purpose of either a class or a race. They must serve him.

We believe that the state cannot possibly be the final teacher of morals. By its very definition the state is an institution based on power; its objectives must be local and provincial. When it subordinates religion to itself it sacrifices its best friend because it forfeits its most disinterested critic. Likewise the state needs the free criticism of the scientist and the educator. It can trust itself with power only as it disciplines itself through free criticism.

To all this those on the eastern side of the line would probably reply:

It is true that Western democracy has given to the vocations, especially those which flourish in the city — money-lending, trading and manufacturing — their greatest opportunity. They have grown strong, but they have grown at the expense of the laborers in the factory and on the farm. The benefits of democracy are one-sided and very limited. Democracy has given to the professions their great opportunity. They have each developed a laudable autonomy. But democracy has not achieved an organic society. Vocational prejudice is almost as acute as class prejudice and race prejudice. The democratic countries are atomistic in their development and unjust in their distribution of rewards.

It is true (those on the east side of the line would say) that education has achieved a remarkable development but this education is practically helpless in the face of great national crises. It does not deal with those issues which are most acute in national life. The universities are filled with loafers to whom education is an opportunity to delve in harmless specialties which have no practical value for suffering humanity. Society must act. It must plan. It must do something about the truth which it possesses. The unlimited accumulation of volumes on library shelves does not justify the vast expenditures on education. Education has not created public-minded citizens.

Those on the east side would continue: The claim that the West worships a God of love in a free church is sheer sentimentality. In the first place, the church is not free.

It is proving itself subservient to the groups who have paid its bills. It has not lifted the ideals of the people to high service in a world of public evil. It has been provincial, interested in self-preservation, filled with competitive strife. It has operated on the low level of the ethics of self-preservation. It has taught private morality in a world of public evil. In the second place, the West has not worshiped a God of love. The God of the West has been a god of power. No nations have more thoroughly followed his bidding than the democratic nations which have ruthlessly penetrated to the uttermost parts of the earth in search of trade. The claim that a God of love is the central idea in Western ethics is hypocrisy. It is well to be rid of such hypocrisy, and this requires that we recognize the sentimentalism and insincerity of all such claims to universality.

Thus, while disclaiming any loyalty to the ideals of democracy, those on the east side of the line would claim that they are creating an organic society in which there is some attempt to solve the problems which democracy has not yet solved. A dictatorship can at least bring order out of chaos. It can plan a totalitarian state which has the machinery for dealing with those large-scale emotions which gather around regional provincialism and class struggle and plague the steps of every Western democratic statesman.

Before this panorama of battling world forces, Western society stands compelled to make some great decisions. In order that it may make them intelligently, it must first reach a better understanding of the past and strive as best it can to envisage the issues involved in various alternatives. The considerations which enter into these great decisions will not be altogether theoretical ones. Ten million unemployed in one nation, with the right kind of leader, may constitute an argument stronger than abstract theory. One thing is certain — humanity is no longer confined to just one way out. Hard-pressed in the midst of a social order which is not providing a satisfactory type of life, Western society now stands at a crossroads where there are multiple alternatives. The remainder of this chapter will be given to a short attempt to explore the road by which we have come and an effort to make clear the issues with which we are confronted.

The thirteenth century has often been called the greatest century in Western social experience. All social forces seemed at that time to be going in the same direction and there was something of a sense of unity of idea and purpose. The West was an organic society. With the growth of the towns and the development of a trader economy this sense of organic unity gave way to that set of ideas which have been grouped under the general concept of democracy. For the past three hundred years we have been emphasizing the rights and responsibilities of the individual. Men began to explore human society almost entirely from this point of view. They developed certain great slogans — the right of private judgment, the right of free speech, freedom of the press, freedom in education, the right of every religious group to organize as it saw fit, private initiative in business and the right of private property. These principles came to be considered as firmly established; they had been won at great cost and seemed to mark out the pathway of all future progress.

But gradually society has taken another turn. Once

more it is beginning to explore the interdependence of life. We are coming to see that the great values of life cannot be gained by individuals who work each for himself. We cannot get married by ourselves, we cannot play baseball by ourselves, we cannot get food by ourselves. We must have cooperative agreements, with their more or less complex regulations. Today collective relationships are more important to us than individual rights and responsibilities. All the various functions of society which have struggled for autonomy are now facing the necessity of deciding how much of their autonomy they must give up in order to establish satisfactory relationships with other functions which are equally necessary to the social body.

Four great experiments are abroad in the world, each of which is characterized by some modification of the principle of autonomy in the vocations. If the Reformation period could be characterized as a period when each of the vocations sought to go its separate way, the present time can be characterized as one in which the vocations are seeking one another for the purpose of effecting an organic interrelationship. The critical question concerns the nature of that relationship. Over against the values of democracy, new movements are stressing the right of the state to coordinate all functions. In economic matters collective control is placed above private control. Education and religion are regimented to make the state more secure. All these new experiments are offering to society some new collective arrangement and they are dealing roughly with the hard-won values and virtues which democracy defends.

It is an interesting fact that the democracies are the first peoples who have ever on a large scale tried to carry on a working society without the help of some powerful idea which stood for the whole as over against the part. The Chinese have a fivefold social order. They tell us the scholar is first because he creates something out of nothing. Next to the scholar comes the farmer because he creates something out of the soil. Next to the farmer comes the mechanic because he creates something with his tools out of wood and iron. Below all these, they tell us, is the trader who simply exchanges products and creates nothing. Last of all, at the bottom of the list, comes the soldier because he only destroys. Whether you like this classification or not, it is a serious attempt to organize functions by awarding them relative places in a hierarchy which establishes status as well as duty.

If you turn to India you have the much discussed caste system. This again is an attempt to provide for national life an industrial regimentation. The Brahman, who is the religious and ethical teacher, worked out the system and naturally placed himself at the top. Next to the Brahman, Indian ideology places the soldier because he controls society by force of arms; he is to the social body what the arms and lungs are to the human body. Below the Brahman and the soldier come the merchants and farmers — those who do the heavy work of the body politic. They correspond to the hips and the legs of the human organism. Last of all come the depressed or outcaste classes to whom is relegated the work which no one else wants to do. Whether you like it or not, such is the framework of the social structure in India. To each caste are assigned both privileges and duties. If you are an outcaste whose duty it is to clean out the latrines and skin the dead cattle, no one is going to take these duties away from you in time of unemployment.

In a similar way medieval Christianity came to terms with the needs of society. It had a caste system of its own which distributed privileges and responsibilities on a somewhat different basis. Its controlling idea was that of the family, within which there were a personal relationship of loyalty and a property relationship of patrimonial proprietorship. Society as a whole followed this pattern. At its head were a feudal lord and an officer of the clergy to whom obedience and loyalty were due. Responsibility in this period meant fidelity to those who were at the top.

But presently something happened to the idea of community and something happened also to the doctrine of responsibility. The various functions of society began to seek what they called autonomy; each attempted to set up in business for itself. Each individual and each group demanded the right to determine what constituted its own welfare and to carry out its idea. The result of this emphasis on the individual part was a failure to set up anything which stood for the whole. The total effect of the Protestant Reformation was the gradual freeing of society from the regimentation of callings organized by the Roman Catholic Church. Whether you tell the story from the economic, the political, the social or the ecclesiastical point of view, the outcome is the same; there gradually disappeared the idea of the organic whole to which the individual part could be loyal.

The society of the last three hundred years stemmed out of a period when the church was dominant over the professions. The church appears as the dark background against which most of the now autonomous vocations have defined themselves, or as the adversary in the struggle of science to cast off the shackles of theology.[2] In their fight to throw off the domination of the church, the various professions and vocations made use of one or other of the various slogans of democracy — free speech, the rights of the individual, freedom of research, economic laissez faire. But important as was this doctrine of freedom, in the course of pursuing it society lost sight of a central concept which gives meaning and purpose to freedom. Of the necessity of some concept which stands for the whole and can come to terms with the part, there seems to be no question.

Faced with the necessity of finding new social forms which will have regard for the common welfare, all the competitors of democracy are making use of the state. Some of them are using the techniques of religion to make the state the object of loyalty. With the glorification of the state has come a waning of interest in the individual and the smaller group. It is assumed that individuals can be propagandized into loyalty, and that the organization of highly propagandized populations into loyalty to the state is an adequate definition of responsibility. The fact that the responsibility must be voluntarily assumed is entirely ignored.

The totalitarian state begins at the outer end of the process. It regiments from the top downward and from without inward. It coordinates all the more delicate phases of life, forces them into the molds which are necessary to the achievements of its totalitarian enthusiasms. Races are brutally treated, families are regimented, and the private world of religion and education is compelled to conform. Instead of being the expression of a rich inward life the state becomes the agent for crushing that life. That is why there is no function so desperately in need of criticism and of free agents of criticism as the political function. Political power is probably the toughest and the most ruthless of all man's power activities. Our only safety lies in subjecting it to unending criticism.

Now there is no reason why the state should not be not only the agent for the control and distribution of power but also the servant of welfare. There does not seem to be any other agency on the horizon which can do the big mass tasks which have to be done. The state can fight famine, poverty, disease, isolation and ignorance. It can control international tariffs, customs and currency rates. Just because it can do these things so well in a world which is just beginning to be conscious of the wide areas that must be discovered and conquered we may expect the state to be increasingly important. Especially in time of crisis men will turn to it.

⤙⤚

Just because the state is taking on these functions the problem of citizenship is now growing acute. Since we are dependent upon the state for so many new services, we must choose our forms of government and our governors with a new sense of their tremendous importance. The time has come for a new dedication of the people to the issues of citizenship. If the state is more and more to be the agent for accomplishing our social purposes, then the exercise of citizenship privileges through faithful and intelligent use of suffrage becomes, next to home life, a cause worthy of our supreme devotion.

The evil of totalitarianism does not lie in either little or much activity on the part of the state. The state's activity, as such, must be judged on its own merits. We might easily decide that a great deal of our common life is now to be organized from political centers. Of course, the tendency to transfer a larger and larger number of activities to the state tends to overamplify the function of the state and to create in it the assumptions of totalitarianism. If we do not want the state to take this role it would be better not to transfer too much power to it.

The evil of totalitarianism lies in the transfer of responsibility from individuals and groups who can and ought to make decisions to some mythical center of responsibility in the state. Democracy, according to Adolf Hitler, wastes the statesman's time in that it compels him to make " the genius of his proposal comprehensible to a flock of silly sheep for the purpose of imploring their final consent." It is in the assumption that the great masses of the people are a flock of silly sheep that the basic evil of totalitarianism lies. For the masses of the people to accept for themselves the role of silly sheep and to transfer their God-given vocation of responsible living to some mythical concept called the state which will relieve them of the task of discovering, defining and defending that which is worthy of supreme devotion — this is an evil which defeats all of life. It is a moral abdication on the part of people in favor of a political leader who will take responsibility for the totality of their lives.

The opposite of totalitarianism is the religious assumption of the worth and dignity of human beings who, under God, feel the necessity of making decisions and of playing a role which is the exact opposite of that of silly sheep. Worship of God carries with it a principle of inward stabilization which releases for service all personal powers, which is the tonic and not the opiate of the people. For both the individual and the group the worship of God may be the beginning of the pilgrimage to spiritual maturity.

Granted all that must be granted about the necessity of a more organic type of society, if that society must be attained at the cost of spiritual and moral creativity on the part of individuals it will be a bigger tragedy than all the failures which can now be chalked up against three hundred years of individualism.

NOTES

1 A summary, taken from the Federal Council Information Service, of an article by Charles E. Merriam in the *Political Science Quarterly* for October 1938.

2 Cf. Andrew D. White, *The History of the Warfare of Science with Theology in Christendom* (New York, D. Appleton Co., 1896).

Christianity and Democracy in the Primary Relationships of Life

The native of New England is attached to his township because it is independent and free; his cooperation in its affairs insures his attachment to its interest; the well-being it affords him secures his affection; and its welfare is the aim of his ambition and of his future exertions: he takes a part in every occurrence in the place; he practices the art of government in the small sphere within his reach; he accustoms himself to those forms which can alone insure the steady progress of liberty; he imbibes their spirit; he acquires a taste for order, comprehends the union or the balance of powers, and collects clear practical notions on the nature of his duties and the extent of his rights.[1]

When De Tocqueville called attention to the family and the township as the communities in which men first learned responsible living, he was anticipating, by almost a century, the observation of the sociologist that communities of primary contacts are the seeding ground of social ethics. The poet in his own way discerns that truth. His praise of the village is more than sentimentality, for he sees in the village the symbol of the primary group relationships which constitute the soil wherein religion and ethics root. His insight is a true one. Villages are the natural " old folk's homes " of the nation, but it is not often recognized that they are also the nurseries of the nation.

The family, and the small community of village and

farm, are the nourishing home of responsible living for people who want to be responsible. There is nothing inherent in these institutions which guarantees responsible living. They can be the places where people cause one another the most intense pain and most thoroughly exploit one another. But if the motives for responsible living are strong, the family and the small community become the first laboratories of citizenship. In the family individuals learn the significance of loyalty to something larger than themselves. The responsibility of the group is distributed among the members, each of whom achieves freedom only by discharging responsibly the functions assigned him.

It is within the family that the mind first forms the images which are basic to its later ideals. The fatherhood of God and the brotherhood of man are concepts which root in family relationships. When people cease to live in families these concepts will mean little or nothing to them.

There are two possible readings of the development of the family from the days of tribalism down to the romantic family of democracy. The way one reads this history will determine somewhat his formula for the improvement of the family in the future.

In the days of tribalism men bought, traded or stole their wives, who more often than not were merely means of increasing the political and economic prestige of the chieftains. Where civilization grows, the tribal family is displaced by the patriarchal family. Here wives are not acquired by barter or theft; they are chosen by patriarchal arrangement. The young groom and bride seldom see each other prior to their wedding day, and after their marriage they go to live in the larger family among the aunts and uncles, the fathers and mothers and other members of the patriarchal household. Very little responsibility rests upon the young people in regard either to the choice of a mate or to the carrying on of their duties as members of the great household.

Higher up on the ladder of civilization appears the family of convention in which marriage is determined by matters of class. There is more freedom of choice on the part of marriage partners but considerations which grow out of the necessity of marrying inside of and for the sake of the state or class are important. Recently a young king set the whole world agog because he refused to marry inside his class. His empire shook with revolutionary convulsions because he disrupted those ordinary procedures which govern the conventional marriage.

Where conditions warrant, the conventional marriage gives way to the romantic marriage to which is attached an economic determinism. This kind of marriage is described most adequately by Bushnell in his " Age of Homespun." [2] He frankly recognizes that the young man chooses his lass because she knows how to spin, because she is frugal, because she is capable of fulfilling the numerous economic functions which were centered in the pioneer home.

The final step in this evolutionary series is the romantic marriage pure and simple. It has its roots in the free association of boys and girls in a coeducational public school system or in some other system which permits abundant opportunity for courtship. That courtship is highly competitive. It is open to both young men and young women. Its boundaries are no longer inside the neighborhood but are extended by ease of communication and transportation. The young people go to live in a small apartment of their own, take full responsibility for all decisions and are expected to be sufficient company for each other. No larger family adds its resources of sociability. No other family in the world starts out with so large a burden of self-support. Many of the functions and services which in the days of homespun centered in the home are performed by the factory, provided the groom — and often the bride — can earn sufficient money to buy them.

Now there are two ways of reading what has happened. To some it seems to have been a continuous pilgrimage in the direction of freedom. They sum up the story with the phrase, " From plunder to courtship." In their view mankind has advanced in a succession of liberations of one part of the family from another, in a continuous enlargement of the principle of liberty and consent. Hence there is but one line of progress for the future. If the democratic family is to be improved it must move in the direction of more and more liberation for its members. There are psychiatrists who would have us believe that once disease is curable, conception preventable, divorce obtainable and God impossible, we will be on the road to complete happiness in marriage. Here the formula is an ever increasing emphasis upon the sacredness of the individual and the importance of human rights. " Give me liberty or give me death " is its intelligent expression in political association.

There is, however, another reading of the history of marriage which holds that the improvement in the relationship of men and women arises from the gradual extension of the role of the man and the woman in a more richly conceived variety of relationships and corresponding responsibilities. Originally there was only one conceivable relationship between man and woman, and that was

the sex relationship.   Whatever men and women did
they did inside of marriage.   But in performing the functions demanded by family life men and women learned to
behave in a variety of ways.   New roles were opened up
to women which required both freedom and responsibility
for their realization.   The employment of women in of-
fices awaited the arrival of women and men who did not
confuse the relationship of employees and employers with
the relationship of husbands and wives.   The nurses in India are not making much progress because Indian public
opinion has not succeeded in understanding that women
in bedrooms can have any other function than that of
wives.   Coeducation was taboo for a long time because people assumed that young men and women in college halls
always behaved as they did in ballrooms.   Freedom of association between men and women has been through
growth of the sense of responsibility and through the discovering and defining of roles which call for discrimina-
tion as to function.

We have advanced from the stage where people live by
force and fear or by custom and rule to the phase where
they live as interacting persons largely because we have become aware of these separate roles which can be defined
and appreciated only by those who have imagination and
who act not according to laws but on the basis of what is
required if they are to fulfill the roles they have accepted.
Freedom, then, is linked with responsibility and a sense of
common welfare.

For those who thus read the history of marriage, improvement of the romantic marriage lies in another direction, that of an increased spiritual maturity and ethical
awareness on the part of all those participating in it.   The

romantic marriage will be improved by a new awareness of the meaning and purpose of the sex function in life. It will be improved by an awareness of what it means to be a person as husband or wife, as son or daughter. It will be improved by a new awareness of the public world to which the family is related on terms of interdependence. As it exists now, the romantic family is often the most selfish family in the world. It enjoys less reinforcement from other great motives, such as loyalty to tradition or country or class, than does any other family, and leaves the two partners with a deplorable poverty of interest. Yet the family which is aware of its dignity and responsibility will fight against any kind of totalitarian state. It will maintain its dignity in the face of intrusion from without. It will not shift the burden of training its children to publicly provided substitutes for father and mother. It will not unnecessarily abandon all the useful arts. To these attitudes it will add a new conviction of the importance of family life for the development of social codes which will make people believe that the building of families and the rearing of children are necessary forms of sacrifice.

The future of the democratic family seems assured. No other institution in society shows any strong tendency to take over the family function. The more one sees of states the more he is satisfied that the extension of the ethics of the state into the circle of the family will be a calamity, whereas the extension of the ethics of the family into the circle of the state will work for social redemption. The democratic family has a real contribution to make to a national culture. It will keep alive in society the deeply rooted values of affection and regard for the individual.

There will be, of course, important functions for the

state to perform. But essentially the family based on affection seems a permanent part of a good society, since the
good society roots in the convictions of those who form
families. The law of the state is force and the law of business is trade and profits; the law of the family is affection
and compassion. Hence the family has a contribution to
make to religion also. When we pray, " Our Father who
art in heaven," we indicate that the basic principle of social
organization is a family principle, one of generosity, of regard for weakness and of tenderness. These words would
become a mere formula were we not continuously experiencing fatherhood, brotherhood and the like within family
relations. Down through the years Christianity has been
sympathetic with the family. Out of the family it has
drawn its great symbols. And in the family men have
learned their greatest ethical lessons. But the lesson they
have learned has not been one primarily of freedom but
rather of freedom to be responsible.

The family, however, is a small-scale community. In the
village and in the township described by De Tocqueville,
the same relationships obtain on a somewhat larger scale.
Here also men experience both freedom and responsibility, and cooperation is invited and rewarded. The township is a comprehensible community. It permits practice
of the art of government in matters which are not too great
for the individual to accomplish successfully. And successful social experience in the smaller areas guarantees both
preparation for and a willingness to attempt adventures in
larger areas.[3]
But there are yet other values to be found in the face-to-

face communities. In the small community life is more plastic than in the great city. Richard Gregg, in a recent magazine article,[4] calls our attention to the " logic of littleness." In expounding this idea he tells us that the small group has a flexibility which it loses as it becomes more ponderous. In large groups there is necessarily a subordination of some to the organizing power of others. Nor is the chance for eliminating bad ideas as great in the large group as in the small. The small group, which calls upon all its members to participate, is much more favorable to that free interchange of ideas which makes for sane and healthy minds.

Several years ago I wrote the following " Code for a Small Community " which presents in more concrete form the attitudes involved in successful primary relationships:

I am one of the smaller communities of America. I am not Chicago and I am not New York. But people come here to exchange the goods of life. Some come here to sell produce and to buy clothing; some come to buy machinery; some come for pleasure; some come for borrowing and lending money; some come for education and some come for religion. Because I am a trade center, therefore I should seek to be a service center.

I will respect myself. I will not indulge in self-pity because I am small.

I will develop and conserve my resources. I will not fail to organize as I should but I will not waste my energy in useless organization.

I will not encourage factional strife of any kind, religious, social or economic. Other communities may be able to endure factionalism but my resources are limited and they must be conserved.

I am a thinking unit in America's great republic which is

ruled by public opinion, and I will endeavor to make my contribution to an intelligent public opinion. I will not knowingly be ruled by ignorance nor prejudice. I will resent all attempts to fill my mind with propaganda as an insult not to be endured at the hands of those who try it.

Because I am a community the most important fact about me is that I have a purpose and a spirit. I will encourage all those individuals and those groups who try to keep their spirit and purpose free from evil and full of righteousness and good will.

I will recognize that probably the basic man in my community is a farmer, a gardener, a fisherman or a miner. Were it not for these people who man the industries, my community would not exist. I will try to prosper with them and not off them.

I am a small community but I do not need to be isolated nor provincial; the goods of the world are mine, but the world expects me to provide as well as take. I will be worthy of the wholehearted devotion of my people because I offer them a chance to secure the abiding satisfactions of life.

The characteristics of the small community which make it the natural home of responsible living and therefore the strategic place for the development of Christian responsible living can be summed up as follows:

Human relationships are simple. The struggle for power is simple and each member can be directly and concretely aware of the total welfare.

Human formulas for the control of power are fairly definite. Between man and woman there is the formula of the good family. Between people occupying contiguous territory there is the formula of the good neighbor. In business dealings there is the formula of the good workman and of business integrity. In discovering the right and wrong of doubtful cases there are the formulas of neighborly justice.

The human situations are comprehensible and the members of the group can use their imaginations in contriving new formulas for adjustment. The mass problems of great populations are utterly bewildering to the individual, but in the simple situations of the small community people of good will can act and see the results of their action. There is the chance for investment of will power and purposive intelligence. Opportunities for selfless devotion and loyalty are abundant. Neighbors meet together and help one another in times of economic need. There is the reward for public-minded service, a reward which expresses itself not in monetary compensation but in the good will and public approval of people in whose eyes a neighbor wishes to be a success.

Now it is my contention that it is the loss of these characteristics, or failure to discover and develop them, which lies at the base of the irresponsible living in the more elaborate and complex situations of modern life. It is true that institutions like the family and the village do not guarantee responsible living. There is a certain illogic to littleness which cannot be overlooked. There is a sense, however, in which a world which has not been subjected to the cash nexus, where people are conscious of one another as persons, constitutes the best opportunity for a society of brotherly men. It is this world which is torn to pieces when men are moved about by the process of buying and selling in the cheapest or highest market without regard to what it does to the human fabric of society. Sir Henry Sumner Maine pointed this out with reference to the Indian village after the industrial revolution had had its way in India.[5] Even with a highly industrialized country like the United States there is a fabric of life which is still immune to the law of the markets. If this immunity is lost, democracy will perish of the totalitarian plague which is spreading over the world.

NOTES

[1] De Tocqueville, *op. cit.,* pp. 67–68.

[2] Horace Bushnell, " The Age of Homespun," *Work and Play* (New York: Charles Scribner's Sons, 1864) , pp. 374–438.

[3] There is today a world-wide renaissance of interest in the family and the village. In India, " village reconstruction " is on the lips of every reformer and statesman. The *ejido,* according to Eyler N. Simpson (*The Ejido,* Chicago: University of Chicago Press, 1937) , offers the basis for the reconstruction of Mexico. Walter A. Terpenning has written a book (*Village and Open-Country Worlds,* New York: Century Co., 1931) enumerating the glories of the European village.

[4] Richard Gregg, " Creative Group Fellowship," *Fellowship,* Oct. 1938.

[5] Henry Sumner Maine, *Village Communities* (New York: Henry Holt & Co., 1889) , p. 192.

Christianity and Democracy in the Public Order

In his book *Village Communities,* Sir Henry Sumner Maine asks the question: " What is the origin of the feeling that it is not creditable to drive a hard bargain with a near relative or friend? " He answers:

The feeling seems to me to bear the traces of the old notion that men united in natural groups do not deal with one another on principles of trade. All indications seem to me to point to the same conclusions: men united in those groups out of which modern society has grown do not trade together on what I may call for shortness " commercial principles."

The general proposition which is the basis of political economy made its first approach to truth under the old circumstances which admitted of men meeting at arm's length not as members of the same group but as strangers. Gradually the assumption of the right to get the best price has penetrated the interior of these groups but is never completely received so long as the bond of connection between man and man is assumed to be that of family or clan connection. The rule only triumphs when the primitive community is in ruins.[1]

The law of the markets then is the assumption that there are areas of life where men deal with one another not as friends nor as members of a family but on the basis of the cash nexus. " As a professional man I refuse to be friends with my clients." So speaks an eminent practitioner. " We do not speak to the people across the hall. We think

85

it small-townish to do so." So the wife of an eminent professor at the University of Chicago describes life in a modern apartment building.

Interestingly enough, modern society has progressed because it has been able to make certain discriminations. The practitioner evidently cannot treat his clients the way he treats the members of his own family. I cannot treat all the people in a department store the way I treat my closest friends. Nothing would be more foolish than for a man to try to greet all the people whom he meets on Michigan boulevard as he greets his friends in the village. Nor does Christian responsibility demand that he should do so. But Christian responsibility does demand that the various relationships of our complex modern society be subject to the law of a total comprehensible good. If I trade with people I must remember that the real object of trade is mutual advantage, not personal profit. If I am elected to political office I must remember that the object of office-holding is the welfare of the people, not personal prestige.

This chapter will attempt to draw up an itemized bill of Christian particulars in the field of the secondary contacts of life. It is not an accident that the rise of the Calvinistic churches, the recognition that man can serve God in his vocation, and the growth of cities were concomitant. The city is the home of the vocations, and the high cost of civilization in an increasingly urban world is the development of a high standard of public-mindedness in vocational groups. Calvinism stressed the idea that a man can exercise his responsibility in the place where he finds himself. Thus Cotton Mather designed an essay upon the good " in a Personal Capacity or in a Relative. Then more particularly unto Magistrates, unto Ministers, unto

Physicians, unto School-masters, unto wealthy Gentlemen and unto several sorts of Officers." [2]

1. Responsibility on the Rural-Urban Highway

There are in the United States approximately 7,300 farm neighborhoods and incorporated and unincorporated small communities having less than 2,500 population. They stand at one end of a rural-urban highway, at the other end of which is the large trade center. To be a democrat means to believe that there can be on this highway a relation of freedom, responsibility and regard for common welfare.

The oldest conflict in the world is the conflict between the city and the hinterland. It is written all through the Old Testament that Hebrew justice was pounded out on the anvil of this struggle. Justice to the poor meant justice to the villager and the villager was the man who did the farming. Most of the achievements of Solomon had back of them conscript labor and a standing army organized to a large extent at the expense of a depressed rural class. Solomon turned over to Rehoboam a country seething with unrest. The peasants' revolt against Rehoboam was a revolt over taxes which Rehoboam promised would be as much heavier than his father's as a man's loins are thicker than his little finger. In Babylon, in Egypt, in Persia there were similar revolts against the cities, which in those early times were largely the strongholds of military and political power. They were called " consuming cities " for they produced none of the necessities of life.

But the modern city of the traders manufactures and produces, and its relationship with the hinterland is supposed to be one of fair exchange and mutual advantage.

Today's urban world needs the raw materials from forest and mine, and food from the farm. It needs the surplus population of the country. It needs also the market which the rural sections offer. And the country needs the products which the city's factories turn out, its banking and professional facilities and for lighter moments the variety and spice its amusement centers afford. The city has what the country needs and the country has what the city needs.

Democracy's formula for the interplay between the rural and urban worlds calls for freedom and cooperation in an interchange of services. But generally the place where those worlds meet becomes a battleground. In the market the farmer bargains with the city over the price of food. In the state legislature he struggles against urban forces over the question of the collection and expenditure of taxes. At the seat of the national government where he meets the trading, manufacturing and money-lending forces the issues have to do with customs, tariffs, currency rates and other forms of government participation in the national economic life. The ethical issues involved in this series of contacts are those of bargaining, the rights of producer, distributor and consumer in what is produced, the distribution and consumption of food, the mutual obligations of creditor and debtor, the stewardship of the land, the profit motive in business and the use of the state to promote public welfare. Historically, the city has been more powerful than the country and has been able to get what it needs by forcible appropriation. It has scarcely recognized the fact that the farmer exercises a great stewardship of the land which he holds in trust to feed the hungry multitudes of the nonfarming population, nor has it realized that free cooperating farmers can make more food available than farmers who are regimented either in a modern totalitarian state or under some ancient feudal regime.

Democracy faces a hard task on the rural-urban highway. It must fight first of all for the right of the farmer to be responsible. It must put into his hands power sufficient to enable him to resist exploiting forces from without. At the same time it must develop in him a sense of responsibility which will make him recognize that he is free only to be a servant of the common welfare. The opposite of a regimented farmer is not an individualistic farmer glorying in the private ownership of his land; it is a responsible farmer freely accepting the stewardship of land as an opportunity for producing food for the city, not because he has to but because he wants to.

But a sense of responsibility at the other end will be still harder to get. There is a tendency on the part of urban forces to assume that they are social ultimates. The urban consumer especially believes that he has a sort of divine right to cheap food, regardless of the conditions under which the food is produced. He fails to recognize that two-thirds of the price he pays at the store represents what the city dealers pay themselves after the food gets inside the city limits. More than that, the city man assumes a divine right to a standard of living which bears no reference to the living at the other end of the rural-urban highway.

Even liberals who have espoused the cause of urban labor and declared that it had a right to orderly bargaining with capital have often turned their backs on the right of the farmer to a just price for the products of his labor. Jane Addams defended the right of union workers to proper hours and wages, but when the farmers went on strike said that for them to withhold food from the hungry millions of the city was one more evidence of their provincialism. One of the tests of democracy will be its ability to include both rural and urban in a total picture of national good.

A vivid memory of my early life in Chicago is of a very good woman who called on the telephone and said, " Dr. Bundesen says that if these farmers out here in the milkshed go on strike it is likely to imperil the purity of our milk supply and endanger the lives of our children." I was stirred by her message. In the course of events, I was made chairman of a committee appointed to hold hearings in the milkshed and find out what the trouble was all about. I found one good woman with four children standing at the telephone twenty consecutive hours directing the picket line of the farmers' strike in southern Wisconsin. She wanted a better standard of life with less drudgery for herself and her family, and this seemed the only way to get it.

Now here were two perfectly good women wanting legitimate things. Here was a simple process organized around a milk bottle, a process so full of turmoil that it was almost impossible for the participants to have really responsible thoughts about it. Thus far there has not been sufficient public-mindedness and social ingenuity to bring democracy along this rural-urban highway.

Let me illustrate my point by an account of certain events relating to Chicago's milk supply. There was a time when Chicago's milk supply was a simple matter. The farmer with a little surplus milk sold the surplus to a neighbor who had not sufficient milk for his needs. The farmer who had the surplus saw to it that his milk was clean because he did not want to be called a dirty neighbor.

The neighbor who bought the milk did not pay too small a price because he did not want to be called a skinflint. And the small boy who delivered the milk behaved himself because he knew he was watched from both ends of the process.

And then, tradition has it, one morning Mrs. O'Leary's cow kicked the lantern over and started a conflagration which consumed the city. And after the city had been rebuilt the city fathers made a law that from that time on no one would be allowed to keep a cow or a goat inside the city limits. Anyone who wanted to keep a cow or a goat had to move to Evanston or points beyond. So the citizens could no longer buy milk from their neighbors. It was delivered by a stranger whom they knew only in his capacity as a deliverer of milk.

Today that first farmer has become eighteen thousand farmers, that neighbor who purchased the milk has become three and a quarter million consumers, and that small boy has become eight thousand milk wagon drivers' union men and one hundred and fifty distributors. And the process of supplying Chicago with milk has frequently been one of conflict — bitter conflict — strikes and lockouts. Some of these one hundred and fifty distributors are financed from a central banking house in New York. (Today four major corporations, financed from New York, control a very large part of the dairy products of the nation.)

Across one counter the corporation has bargained for the products of the farmer and across another counter it has bargained for labor. It has always been advantaged when there were three laboring men standing at the gate bidding for a job which required only one. It has always been advantaged when there have been five quarts of milk coming to a market which demanded only one. And the managers of these corporations have understood not only how to restrict competition for themselves; they have been equally adept at multiplying competition among the laborers and among the farmers.

One result of the corporations' tactics is the large number of desperately driven farmers on the great plains of the United States. During one of the milk strikes in Chicago the manager of perhaps the most important of the big distributing companies told me: " These farmers are foolish. They can't control the market. There are twenty-two different railroads coming into the city of Chicago. We have our glass-lined tank cars; we can bring in milk on every one of those railroads and we can bring it in from Oregon or from Texas. We have the situation completely in our control. There is only one thing for the farmer to do and that is to beat his fellow farmer in competition."

And of course labor is in the same situation. There are eight thousand men in the milk wagon drivers' union of Chicago. There are fifty thousand men who would like those jobs. The union has had to protect itself by every means in its power. And the gangster has long since seen that such a situation spells opportunity for him. Chicago is notorious for the extent to which gangsters have controlled its unions, but in the case of the milk wagon drivers' union they met their match.

Old Steve Sumner, who organized the milk wagon drivers' union in Chicago, himself told me the story of a historic battle with the gangs — in 1932, about the time Chicago was beginning work for the Century of Progress exposition. One day Murray Humphrey, a representative of Al Capone's gang (for Al himself was on his way to Alcatraz) , came into Steve's office, saying, " Steve, we want to put a man in this office."

Steve asked, " What's the matter, Murray, do you want a job? "

Humphrey replied, " No, we want a man in this office, and for every wagon you've got on the streets of Chicago you will pay three dollars a week into our gang. We will guarantee you protection. We will guarantee that you have a monopoly on the jobs of the milk wagon drivers' union in this city."

Steve Sumner answered him: " Murray, I was the organizer of this union. I am eighty-three years old and if you get into this office you will get in over my dead body."

Murray shrugged his shoulders. " Steve, there was a time when we didn't use machine guns."

" Murray, there was a time when we didn't either," Steve retorted.

Murray left the office. The next day the president of the milk wagon drivers' union was kidnaped, and it cost Steve Sumner fifty thousand dollars to get him released. Then the gang informed Steve Sumner that he was the next man on the spot. Steve's answer to that was: " Boys, this is going to be a war." He laid his plans. The next Sunday he went to union headquarters and made an announcement to the members. " If we're going to have a war," he said, " let's make this a real war. Let's make it such a war that the whole city will know what is happening in this devilish competitive game." And he outlined his plans to them.

So they told him to go ahead and set about fortifying the milk wagon drivers' headquarters. He covered the windows with bullet-proof steel mesh. In the back of the

assembly room he built a booth — something like the
booth in the back of a movie theater — where he posted a
man armed with a gun to keep guard over every office on
the first floor of the building.   He bullet-proofed the walls.
He established a man with a machine gun across the street.
He bought Mr. Insull's old armored car (which Mr. Insull
had no need of just then because he was in Greece) and the
union officials went back and forth between home and
headquarters in it.   The newspapers caught the implication of the union's moves and played up the story.

I saw Steve the next week.   He said: " Mr. Holt, I just
saw old Fort Dearborn that they put up as a part of the
Century of Progress celebration.   Those boys back there
didn't know what trouble was.   What they really ought to
do is to take this contraption that we built here and put
it alongside old Fort Dearborn and write over it all, ' A
Century of Progress '! "

Did Steve Sumner and his union have an opportunity to
be public-minded?   Did the farmers who kept any milk
from coming into Chicago have an opportunity to be public-minded?   No!   Property-mindedness on the part of one
group made class-mindedness on the part of the other two
groups.   That result was inevitable; there was no way of
escaping it.   Each group was exactly as public-minded as
the other two, and so all were forced to forget the fact that
the reason for supplying the city with milk was, after all,
to save the health of little children.   This story of the
breakdown of public-mindedness in one industry illustrates what has happened all along the rural-urban highway.

It would, however, be unfair to classify as evil-minded
all the groups which participate in this process.   It is not

alone a matter of the will to be good. The original farmers' organization took as its slogan: " We will supply Chicago with pure milk, not because we have to but because we want to." Here was corporate public-mindedness. Nor are all the companies that distribute milk in Chicago controlled by a New York banker's demand for his five per cent. But it becomes increasingly clear that true public-mindedness cannot be achieved apart from an organization of producer, laborer, distributor and consumer which shifts the goal of the process from profit to public service.

This does not necessarily mean that the City Hall should turn the business of supplying Chicago with food into a publicly owned utility. Probably nothing could be worse. Public ownership does not necessarily mean socialization. In South Africa the government owns the railroads and the steel mills and it is perfectly evident that this is simply one way in which the white population makes use of government ownership to control the black population. Public ownership does not mean socialization until we know who controls the government. If the people of Chicago to-day were to vote on the price of milk as they vote on a streetcar franchise there is little doubt that the farmer would be worse off than he is at present.

However, these considerations do not obscure the fact that some kind of relationship must be established which makes it safe for each group to surrender its present selfish and militant attitude in the confidence that it is enlisting for public service. Someone remarked that gang life will disappear from Chicago when the government steps in and actually performs the service which the gang, in a very selfish way, offers to perform. It is true that a " century of progress " has resulted in a situation where all groups in society operate more like gangs than like public service agents. These gangs will not surrender until there is something representing the general welfare to which they can surrender. The war on the rural-urban highway will not end until all those little armies can rally around one flag. The problem of vocational and professional ethics is largely the problem of making it possible for these little conspiracies against the public to surrender to something which more thoroughly serves the public.

2. Can the Professions be Centers of Public-Mindedness?

There are five great professions which are older than the state: law, medicine, journalism, teaching and religion. They have maintained a high degree of professional discipline and have fought great battles for human welfare. To believe in democracy is to believe that these professions can keep their freedom without becoming conspiracies against the public. I hold that teachers know more about teaching than politicians can ever know, that journalists are justified in demanding freedom of the press because of the good results that freedom has yielded in the past. I believe that doctors know more about what makes for public health than any other group and I would fight for the separation of the church from the state and for the freedom of the clergy. But the fact remains that because of professional pride and avarice, these great professions are not giving to the public the service it has the right to demand. Democracy's competitors are at the door and they are in no mood to wait for these groups to make up their minds to be centers of public service. Only a moral revolution in their own ranks can save the professions from regimentation. State control and regimentation would undoubtedly be a calamity but unless the professions choose to be voluntary centers of public-minded effort they will be regimented by the state.

When Andrew D. White, in 1896, published his book, *The History of the Warfare of Science with Theology in Christendom,* he set up the Magna Charta of the various professions. Hitherto they had been dependent upon theology for their sanctions. One by one White told the stories of how the various branches of science — geography, astronomy, anthropology, psychology, medicine — had fought their way free from the limitations placed upon them by the theologians. The tale of the physician who justified the use of anaesthetics in obstetrical operations by proving that, when Eve was taken from the body of Adam, God caused a deep sleep to fall upon Adam, is a fair sample of the methods the learned professions had to use in their struggle against theological opposition. It is a story which is not creditable to theology. But one issue, and perhaps the most important, White neither raised nor answered: the question of what these learned professions were going to do with their newly found autonomy and prestige; whether they would be little conspiracies against the public or centers of public-minded service and public-minded thinking for a total welfare. This was a question religion had raised and had in its own way answered. But when the professions achieved autonomy too many of them ceased to ask it.

The principle of autonomy has brought about the functional separation of education, medicine, law, journalism and the church. Each operates independently, with little or no regard to what any of the others is doing. Each is conscious only of its self-chosen goals and pursues them with an energy never before known in human history. Religion itself, freed from association with the state and from other phases of social life, has probably more vigorous representation today than ever before. The churches in the United States at least are proud of their separation from the state. They are older than the state and they live in the voluntary loyalty of people. All these positive gains in the professions under the principle of autonomy it is necessary to record.

But it is necessary to record the losses also. The great loss attending the professions' achievement of autonomy is an increasing vagueness in any thought which stands for the whole of society as the church once stood in the Middle Ages. Society has no center recognized as such by all its parts. Today the great self-conscious professional groups, ambitious for their prestige and power, contend stubbornly, each for its own vested interest, and fail utterly to think in a public-minded way of a total human welfare. Education is conducted not with a view to the whole man but rather for the glory of that particular fragment of culture which any department represents. The principle of freedom of the press is made to justify the newspaper's behaving in a way that brings rewards to the newspaper but has slight regard for public welfare. And the professions indulge their jealousy of one another. There is not a great deal of race prejudice on a university campus but there is an enormous amount of interdepartmental prejudice. Nor are the church and the clergy public-minded. Churches are perfectly willing to crucify communities on the cross of denominational glory.

It is not surprising that of late, both within and without the professions, there has been a growing demand for rec-

ognition of a sense of community which will answer the
question, What is the purpose and the end of all our autonomy?   For what greater good do these self-conscious
professional groups exist?   Once again there is a reaching
out for that larger thought which stands for society as a
whole.   Inside the professions the movement takes such
form as the various dinner clubs whose slogan is, " He profits most who serves best."   The ritual and the general emotional behavior of these groups make them nothing short of
a layman's religion which is capturing the loyalty of millions of men who sit around dinner tables and listen to in-
terminable speeches about the public welfare.   Outside
the professions there are movements which emphasize and
symbolize the total welfare as the object of obligation on
the part of professional groups.   Men are asking questions
about the health of all the people and are beginning to
speak of socialized medicine.   The community church has
its advocates, and there is talk about the religion which is
outside the church and not subject to the limitation of the
old forms.   Above everything else men are looking to the
state as the new form of community which represents all
of us.

But is this sense of community to be forced down upon
us from the top, or self-imposed and defined through public-minded thinking on the part of the various professional
groups?   Socialization is inevitable.   But is it to be socialization through compulsion or socialization through democratic, ethical action?

Nothing could be further from good policy in seeking to
recover responsible living in the United States than to look
to government regulation as a source of such living.   Unless there are large groups whose public-mindedness rests

on a deeper foundation than government regulation there is little hope for freedom in the future. It would seem that if this foundation can be discovered anywhere it is in these great professional groups whose tradition of service runs far back in history and who have, in the United States, large resources for responsible living. The question we face, then, is whether or not professional consciousness can be a reliable source of public-mindedness. Can these major vocational groups — clergymen, teachers, lawyers, doctors and journalists — muster the attitudes which will enable them to take the lead? These are issues which bring a sense of crisis to the individuals in the professions who must face them. There is a high road and a low road. We are moving in the direction of discovering these issues when we realize that, of every profession, there are questions to be asked as to its control and purpose and that this control and purpose have significance for the wills of those who share in the vocation. Of every community of utility it is proper to ask, What useful purpose does it serve and do those who participate in it cooperate for the realization of that purpose? For instance, do those who are members of the legal profession seek to promote law and justice or have they focused their minds on the monetary returns from the vocation? Again, every vocation involves certain relationships among the people who carry it on. What is the social arrangement among these people?

The attitudes which the professions must develop if they are to lead in the quest for responsible living are not wholly different from those which characterized individuals in the simple face-to-face relationships of the small community. They are, first, a sense of interdependence based on awareness of a total welfare; second, fairly definite formulas for good and bad behavior in the various professional groups; third, a system of recognition for good conduct and condemnation of bad conduct; fourth, the continuous envisioning through the imagination of conceivable formulas for public-minded behavior. All these attitudes, be it noted, are based on moral insights.

In the attempt to develop these attitudes there will be a minimum of reliance upon the state for the defining and defending of good conduct. A larger reliance will be placed upon the powers of the group spirit, informed and defined by great personalities in the various vocations who make excellence real and desirable. A sense of this excellence will be kept alive by the celebration of great occasions when, by remembrance, recognition, ritual and codes, the group spirit will be directed along lines of public-mindedness. There will be schools for vocational training which hand on the accumulated skills of the vocation but also seek to transfer the spirit of public-minded conduct. These schools will be open only to persons carefully chosen for their natural aptitude for the profession in question.

In his description of the good physician Dr. Richard Cabot sums up the qualities of the public-minded professional man. The good physician, he says, will have the exploring instinct. He will answer the challenge of the unknown. He will be characterized by a certain austerity. His mind will develop resistance to common fallacies and easy generalizations. He will have the desire to make a living and the desire for a reputation but these will always be tempered by the desire to use his powers altruistically. He must be satisfied with modest monetary rewards and care more for those psychic rewards which come in the gratitude of the patient and the approval of society. He must combine in himself the peacemaker, the teacher and the leader. Back of all these will be his appreciation of the Christian motives that make for the satisfaction of deep and permanent desires in ourselves and others, not merely of obvious desires.[3]

Here is the statement of one of a class of young clergymen which attempts to itemize the ministry's obligations to be true to itself and to the larger public:

As a clergyman I recognize the uniqueness of my vocation as the interpreter of all other vocations in the light of God's eternal purpose for a divine community here on earth.

I will take my place in the historic line of interpreters of the Christian faith. I expect to share their fate. I hope to increase their prestige. I will honor and exalt all who have made the name of this vocation glorious.

As an American clergyman, I must operate under the conditions imposed by the separation of church and state. I am dependent on the voluntary giving of people. I will not waste the resources placed at my disposal. I will maintain my freedom from the state, foregoing all state support. I will be open and frank in all my business dealing, especially with my church.

I will work to increase the number of educated clergy, by disciplining my own mind, by encouraging all means by which educational advantages are placed at the disposal of clergymen.

I will defend the right of the minority group in religion but I will encourage with equal courage all efforts to bring unity of mind and effort among Christians.

I will be loyal to my group by accepting the humble obligations of a parish ministry but I will seek to lead my people in public-minded service to the whole community.

I recognize the validity of non-Christian faiths and will seek to understand them and to work in fellowship with them.

In so far as it is consistent with the encouragement of good work on the part of all clergymen I will work for and accept a basic salary scale for all. Whatever special gifts or concessions are made, such as special discounts, railroad concessions, etc., I should prefer to have made to the church rather than to myself, hoping that my church will pay such a salary as will remove from me the need for any concessions.

I believe it is my duty to understand the moral phases of public questions and to use my influence to build a right public opinion.

I recognize the obligation to do my own thinking. If I use the results of the thinking of other men I will give due credit for the same. I will guard all confidences entrusted to me as sacred.

I will not undermine by gossip or by any other method the work of a brother minister.

If called upon to render service in another parish I will consult the minister of that parish before so doing.

I will seek to enlarge and enrich my services of public worship.

I will respect and honor the vocations other than that of the ministry of religion. In them I see the chance for men to honor God in their " callings." In the community I see the framework in which these vocations are to be carried on, and the chance to build the community of God on earth.[4]

If attitudes such as those of this young clergyman or of Dr. Cabot's good physician were shared by all the members of professional groups, the problems that face American democracy would be well on their way to solution. Can the professions be centers of public-mindedness? I believe that they can. And I know that if they do not choose to accept the responsibility for which their traditions fit them they will be regimented and democracy will be on the way to defeat.

3. Can Class-Conscious Groups Become Public-Minded?

John Calvin, laissez faire and the discovery of new land released more forces in the world than society has ever been able to control for the public good. In accordance with the principles of laissez faire, freedom was given to industry in the confident belief that each man would best serve the state by pursuing his own welfare. It gradually became apparent, however, that five selfish men, each pursuing his own welfare, do not arrive at common welfare. Largely as a result of the failure of laissez faire the totalitarian governments have arisen, which assume that industrial power can be so directed by the state that common welfare will be achieved. They embrace the other extreme. Democracy's idea however lies somewhere between.

In the two hundred counties of the United States which stretch between the Mississippi river and the Atlantic seacoast along the bays of the Great Lakes are the headquarters of two hundred corporations that own 50 per cent of the country's nonbanking wealth and employ 75 per cent of its industrial labor. To believe in democracy means to believe that it is possible to distribute among their workers more and more of the power of these two hundred corporations, and to believe that after labor has taken increasing control it will not turn around and exploit the agricultural hinterland even more severely than the predatory-minded bourgeoisie has done. This is democracy's major adventure in faith, ethics and social organization, and it must be captained by the workers themselves. Like the professions, business faces state regimentation unless it permits the class-consciousness it has unintentionally but inevitably fostered to become the new basis of public-mindedness. Can this be accomplished? Can freedom, responsibility and regard for common welfare grow along the highway which leads from the factory to the public?

It would be pleasant if we could record that, as a result of moving from home production and neighborhood consumption to high-powered production in factory and on farm, we had moved to a well ordered group organization of traders, farmers, laborers and consumers, all functioning now as public-minded groups anxious to serve the common welfare. Actually, however, there would be little realism in such a picture.

For two hundred years we have lived in a trader-controlled world. For two hundred years the basic processes of raw material production, conversion and sale have been planned and directed by traders. The story takes us a long way back in history. I have already referred to the English merchant seamen who three hundred years ago ventured out on the seven seas and by their courage and skill lifted England to the leading place in world commerce. These men had a sense for navigation; they knew the significance of tariffs, customs and currency rates; and John Calvin had taught them that it was right to take interest and trade for profit. They were more pious than saintly. Sir John Hawkins carried slaves from Sierra Leone to Spain in a ship called the *Jesus of Lubeck* and he counseled his crews to " serve God daily; love one another; preserve your victuals; beware of fire, and seek good company."

These merchant seamen founded such centers of trade as Boston, New York and Philadelphia. Here for a hundred and fifty years their sons carried on and then, because they also had a sense for navigation, tariffs and currency rates, they staged a revolution against the traders of the home country. According to Charles A. Beard the issues were: (1) navigation acts, (2) laws restricting freedom of trade, (3) restriction of colonial manufacture, (4) currency rates favorable to the creditor class, and (5) taxation without representation — all causes dear to the trader heart.[5] Emerging successfully from the war of the Revolution this trader class with the aid of Alexander Hamilton and John Marshall firmly established themselves at the center of the new government. Then they began to advantage themselves by favorable customs, tariffs and currency rates. The agricultural south protested and in the second great war of the nation was beaten to earth.

What our trader class had tried to do on a national scale their brothers in other nations had tried to do on an international scale and the World War came as the culmination of the world-wide ambitions of those who ruled from the port cities on the seven seas. Into this war our own world traders dragged us. It was a devastating conflict, but out of it we emerged as we entered, industrial-end foremost. At the close of the boom period which followed the war James W. Gerard could say that fifty-nine men controlled America, and the only protest so far registered is from a few who were disturbed because they had not been listed among the fifty-nine. Berle and Means give us a more factual picture of the situation.[6] They describe the two hundred corporations which own most of the tools of production and over half the nonbanking wealth of the United States. The territory which they occupy has the greatest concentration of population in the country, publishes most of the newspapers, loans most of the money and elects most of the presidents.

When the trader class tells the story of its own success, it tries to create the impression that its strength is the result of the " rugged individualism " it has upheld. But as a matter of fact no other class has been the recipient of so many special privileges. Its success is owing not so much to rugged individualism as to the fact that it has carried a bag of tricks. It has bargained across two counters, over one with the workman for his labor and over the other with the farmer for his raw materials. In both these bargaining operations it has been clever enough to limit competition among its own members and multiply competition among those on the other side of the counter. If we examine this bag of tricks we shall find five major ones.

First is the advantage which those at the center of society always have over those at the circumference — that of quick information and ready conference, and the means and ability to play off against one another the groups on the margin.

Second, from the beginning the trader class have been the creditor class and they with their spiritual abettors have kept alive an enthusiasm for debt-paying as a religious obligation. They have never been concerned to discover whether their system for getting people into debt was valid. Any debtor who objected to paying his debt with a dollar whose value had doubled since the debt was incurred they declared to be a repudiator of honesty and a moral outcast.

Third, this class has written the country's tariff laws and thus created a situation where its bargaining power was almost double that of the farmer with whom it bargained. The farmer has sold in a world market and bought in a protected market. The tariff has cost him eight dollars to every dollar it has made for him.

Fourth, the traders have written most of the tax laws of

the country and thus have succeeded in putting an undue
burden on the owner of tangible real estate. Taxes ab-
sorb seven per cent of urban net rent and thirty-five per
cent of rural net rent.

Finally, these men have voted themselves unbelievably
large rewards for doing the things which traders do. Their
incomes make the kings of the feudal ages look like poverty-stricken beggars, and are out of all proportion to any
possible service the recipients can render society. One of
the trader class was recently appointed a receiver of three
defunct banks in which poor depositors lost millions. For
a few months' work the receiver was allowed a salary of
fifty-seven thousand dollars. A group of real estate men
who some time ago carried through a fairly simple plan for
the transfer of certain land to the city of Chicago charged a
commission which ran into the millions for each member
of the firm. The professional men who associate with the
traders place the same high valuation on their own services.
The idea that these men earn the sums at which they value
their services is a fiction believed only by the simple-
minded.

But even more important, these men and their kind,
their families and their children, set the standards of living and the ethical goals of society. In that magnificent
book *The Epic of America,* James Truslow Adams describes the moral debacle which took place when, about
the middle of the last century, money-making as an end
in itself displaced the dream of the welfare of the common
man as the goal of American society.

The social effects of the rule of the trader class are not
easy to summarize. It would be foolish to deny the benefits that have resulted from that rule — the growth of sci-

ence, the uniting of the world if not in brotherhood at least in neighborhood, the marvelous victory over time and space accomplished through the use of steamship, railroad, airplane, telegraph and radio. It has been the mission of the trader to tie the world together in a great web of commercial interrelations.

But the items on the debit side of the ledger must not be missed. The trader has promoted competition between and within rural classes and urban labor. The rural north and the rural south have voted against each other for the last fifty years. Urban classes have kept alive and promoted the tradition of rural individualism. The trader has fostered overamplification of what men do in cities. The size and opulence of the city are out of all proportion to its usefulness. Again, the trader is responsible for the distortion of the picture of the nation's total welfare. Our notion of what business is for is entirely askew. We have thought it sufficient that men should grab out of it under the guise of profit whatever they could get. Profit-grabbing has become synonymous with business and business men have been interested only in making their profit no matter what happened to trade and commerce as a whole. Much less have they been concerned with the effect of their attitude in other places. The moral bankruptcy of the business world has infected and corrupted every other field of life, even religion.

The world around, two great classes are seething with revolt: the farming population and the urban proletariat. In Russia it was the farmers who joined with the urban proletariat to overthrow the trader class of the cities. The uprising in India is a revolt of the villages against the domination of the port cities. In Denmark, the transition to an order in which the farmer participates with self-respect has already been made. An enraged rural class has been the driving power behind many of the upheavals in the western hemisphere. The end of the feudal era saw the urban classes in revolt; the end of three hundred years of urban control of Western civilization witnesses the mutterings of revolt on all the great agricultural plains of the world.

It would be nice if we could record that in this three-cornered struggle for power between trader, farmer and laborer the government has always sought to exercise its authority in the interests of the total national good. Realism compels us to record that the government has generally been captured by the dominant party in the conflict and has been an accessory to the power of the traders rather than its master.

It would be nice if we could record that the church has spoken with equal emphasis to each of these warring parties, as it did in the days when the struggle was simple. Realism compels us to record such facts as that, in the time of Alexander Hamilton and Thomas Jefferson, the actions of the Connecticut clergy justified the reproach that they were the " Cossacks of the Federalist party "; and that, in the conflict between Jackson and Adams, the clergy joined the bankers in supporting Adams. The Populist struggle which culminated in the battle between Bryan and McKinley found the metropolitan clergy — Catholic, Jewish and Protestant, from Chicago to the Atlantic seacoast — voting the way Mark Hanna wanted them to vote. The verdict against the church is clear.

Neither the government nor the church has acted responsibly. Where then is to be found the leadership which will put an end to the industrial struggle that has again and again torn the United States, even to the extent of disrupting the Union?

First of all let us affirm that the motive which has lain back of the industrial process is utterly bad. It has never been mitigated by that commitment to service which has often characterized the professions. To believe that, out of the process by which people get their daily bread, it is right for a man to grab what he can as legitimate reward for his activities is to put the whole industrial system beyond the realm of morals. Selfishness multiplied a thousandfold never produces public-mindedness. Nothing but a moral revolution at this point can reconstruct the industrial world.

Again, let us affirm that a system which awards to the entrepreneur all that is left after he has paid for raw materials and labor and met tax and interest charges, encourages, even compels him to drive a hard bargain, to pay the lowest wages possible and to buy in the cheapest market he can contrive to create. This puts a strain on human character that it ought not to be subjected to.

Let us affirm, in the third place, that concentration of an entire nation's tools of production in the hands of a few of its members cannot be justified any more than can the concentration of land ownership in the hands of a few feudal lords in a country like Mexico. The same considerations which caused the United States to democratize the laws of landholding obtain in the case of the tools of production. Ownership of tools must be distributed among those who use the tools.

How are the workers who produce to acquire a share in the means of production? The question of method is of vast importance, for the method by which power is acquired and distributed generally determines the way in which it is later used. Power won by violent means is likely to be exercised violently. Force begets force. In a recent article in the *Atlantic Monthly*, Bertrand Russell discusses the implications of power won by violence for the world as a whole.[7] The burden of his discussion is that liberty and a sense of responsibility cannot grow out of war. War always results in something quite different from what was fought for. The American people need hardly be reminded of that; they have learned by bitter experience that a war to make the world safe for democracy ends in democracy's utter defeat. But they need to be reminded that the same truth holds on a small scale also. If labor employs force to obtain control of the tools of production it will neither distribute them justly nor use them with regard for the total welfare. The dictatorship of the urban proletariat will not issue in a world of freedom and justice any more than did the dictatorship of landowners or of traders. When class consciousness takes possession of men the standard of good conduct falls before the urges of class pride and class hatred.

The primary question in the socialization of economic power is not whether it is to be distributed through political arrangement or through appropriation by mass action. The primary question is one of psychological attitudes, and this is the field in which religion and ethics operate. But there can be no ethics without power, hence power must be returned to the disinherited and power must be taken from those who have appropriated more than their share of it. Let us frankly affirm that the organization of farmer, laborer and consumer into their respective groups is to be encouraged. But let us affirm also that groups must yield to the obligation of asking what they should do in order to promote the world of brotherly men.

There are those who would solve the problem by taking power away from all industrial groups and transferring it to the government. The government would add to its political power the economic power of farmer, laborer, trader and consumer. But this solution simply shifts the economic struggle to the political field. The men on opposite sides of a bushel of wheat or the consumer-producer problem carry their struggle to the seat of government. New kinds of tricks are devised, economic revolt becomes treason to be dealt with by military means. Such a concentration of power at political centers is bad for both government and economics.

Another solution calls for a coalition of the farmers and the laborers to displace the present trader control through some kind of revolutionary action. But action of this kind does not seem to provide the psychological basis for good action later on. As we have already pointed out, violent seizure of power does not result in a reign of justice.

There is another solution to the problem of the socialization of economic power, one I believe to be truly democratic and responsible. It recognizes distinct separation of function as between government, economic agencies and cultural agencies. The government remains an agent for socialization, but with an increasing awareness of the ways in which it could be captured by powerful economic groups. The economic groups are organized, but they recognize their obligation to make their class-consciousness the adolescent stage of a new public-mindedness. They believe that the system of production, manufacture and consumption exists for the common welfare and not for private profit. They understand that they are parts of an interdependent process and that no one group may seek success at the expense of the others — indeed, ultimately cannot succeed without the others. Cultural agencies like the church and the school are also free but recognize their obligation to speak to all groups about that larger good which is inclusive enough to be worthy of the public-minded devotion of each. That larger good is always changing; there is no final statement of it. But whatever its specific form at any given moment it presupposes the cohesive loyalty of brotherly action.

4. Moral Sentiment and the Modern State

Democracy's competitors, faced with the necessity of finding new forms of community, are turning with enthusiasm to the state. Their enthusiasm is not entirely unreasonable. The state is one of the most useful instruments forged by modern man. But aside from the fact that it encourages idolatrous worship of itself, the totalitarian state tends to foster irresponsibility by making it easy for its people to slip into the philosophy of " let the state do it." It is quite possible to recognize the importance of the state and yet count as gain every center of responsibility which carries its own burden independently. To this theory democracy strongly clings.

It is foolish to ignore the fact that the state does many things well. Only the state is powerful enough to act in the face of a great famine. Only the state can muster the police force and introduce the sanitary measures to which epidemics succumb. Only the state can undertake the great engineering projects — the building of harbors, the widening of rivers, the construction of dams — which make ocean transportation possible and make the inland streams our servants. Henry Ford builds a good automobile but he operates it on state-provided highways. Research and publication by the state make available to all the people the wisdom of the scientist. Private institutions educate a certain proportion of our people but mass education is carried on through the public schools and the state universities. Through the state social services far beyond the limits of private charity are extended to the needy of the city and the great hinterlands.

But the fact that the state is better able to give services of this nature than any other available agency is no reason for letting the state " do it all." Indeed certain considerations suggest that such wholesale turning over of power to the state is highly dangerous. Historically the state in the modern sense is an agency for the control of social forces. Its origins can be traced to the days when the burghers, the traders who dwelt in cities, began to preempt the power which had hitherto been in the hands of the feudal lords. The modern state had its inception as an agency for the control of a burgher society, presumably in the interest of the general welfare. The burghers, however, looked after themselves. They permitted the state to create the army but they decided what the army should do. With the ships and arms and men furnished by the new governments the traders of western Europe set out to capture for their respective states the natural resources and the native peoples of the far lands east and west. Thus the state became the agent of those who stood at the projecting end of empire. And one cannot but admit that its accomplishments have been tremendous.

There are, however, certain functions which the state

does not perform well, and if we read correctly the lessons of the past there are other functions which it is not likely to perform well.   When it attempted to organize those matters of conscience which demand freedom and a certain amount of isolation, the state behaved badly.   Religion and the state, when either is directly under the control of the other, tend to corrupt each other.   The same will probably be true in matters of education where issues are critical.   A prominent educator not long ago remarked that for a hundred years education has been busy at the task of freeing itself from religion, and that it will probably have to spend the next hundred years freeing itself from the state.

The world of primary contacts, such as the relationships within families and neighborhoods, is all the better for being free from state control.   Indeed regimentation here would work irreparable damage.   In a democracy rule must be by majorities even though society does not advance majority-end foremost.   But if majorities undertook to regulate the primary contacts they would probably crush out the spontaneity of those delicate phases of life which do not await the adoption of a constitution and by-laws.

Again, to deliver to the political power the responsibility for all the functions of society will not guarantee that all the social functions will be well performed.   If both political and economic power is lodged in the same officials, the temptation to capture this power will be overwhelming and the exercise of such power will leave much to be desired.   The Amana community in Iowa separated the political, religious and economic functions, because, they said, good deacons did not necessarily make good business managers.   The early members of a totalitarian church in Massachusetts gave up the law which made citizenship dependent on church membership because they had discovered that good church members did not necessarily make good Indian fighters.

Finally, the state, which is the power that makes war, will always tend toward totalitarianism. In times of crisis it regiments both the emotions and the resources of the people. Its tendency to organize the economic resources, and especially to be the agent of empire capitalism, multiplies the situations in which it may seem necessary to declare war. But once the state has declared war it must mobilize all the resources — religious, educational and economic — and such mobilization creates the totalitarian state. The process is cumulative and self-accelerating.

Democracy has proceeded on the theory that in separation of functions there is safety and power. It now faces the necessity of proving that cooperation freely entered into can achieve a more enduring union than can issue from cooperation enforced by the state.

Nevertheless, in spite of all that can be said about the limitations of the modern state, the inevitability of the state's increasing importance must be recognized. New social needs and situations have arisen, and in regard to these we do not know what the state does well and what it does not do well. We must be prepared to explore in these regions. But two convictions are borne in upon the student of the state. The first is that there are several kinds of activities which the state seems to perform well. These can be itemized as follows:

(1) Long-time activities, such as reforestation, which do not return immediate profit though their ultimate returns are immeasurable. (For instance, it is an interesting fact that most of the great breeds of cattle in this country bear

the name of some old feudal lord who had the opportunity to develop his stock through specialized breeding over a long term of years. Work of this kind is now being taken up by state agricultural colleges in state-owned herds.) (2) Large-scale activities like mass education, the burdens of which are entirely too heavy for private forces. (3) General activities that make for public welfare, such as prevention of disease, guaranteeing of social security and large-scale relief, road-building and mail-carrying. Some of these the state has carried on for many years. (4) Activities which have to do with law and order.

There are, on the other hand, activities which the state does not seem to perform so well: (1) Activities which call for special professional skill and devotion. (2) Activities which demand extraordinary personal devotion, such as the responsibilities of parents. (3) Education which is above the average in its experimental quality. (4) Business ventures which offer returns but require unusual initiative. (5) Matters of conscience which involve regimentation of private habits. (A good illustration of this category is the prohibition activities of the state, which ran far ahead of local public sentiment. On the other hand, what the state has accomplished in the way of encouraging local temperance seems to have been good.)

At the present time no one knows just where the line is to be drawn which separates private initiative and state activity. We can advance only in an experimental way.

The second conviction which is borne in upon one is that the state ought not to assume the characteristics of a moral ultimate. Yet at the same time we must recognize that the state does not exist apart from the large-scale emotions and the moral convictions of the people. This is especially true in a democracy. Democracy presupposes a people spiritually mature and ethically aware, able to exercise that criticism without which it cannot live. Democracy assumes the existence of a moral order which deals with matters that are more fundamental than political action. On the hither side of all political action there are great moral convictions which can and must be cultivated.

Robert Owen, the greatest prophet of his day, believed that a new social order was just around the corner provided intelligent men set themselves to planning for it. But he recognized a great obstacle to his plans — prejudice. In his invitation to the public to a convention for discussing a new social system, which appeared in the *New York Tribune* for September 25, 1845, he warns all to leave their prejudices at home. An exact quotation may be in point:

. . . but let everyone endeavor to repress, on this occasion, his own prejudices of locality and the prejudices of others; for it is these early imbibed prejudices alone that now stand between man and a high degree of physical and mental excellence, and progressive happiness in proportion as this excellence shall be attained.

But let none suppose that they are not prejudiced. The people of all nations over the world are locally prejudiced — in their sectarian dissensions, in their laws, governments and customs, in their classifications and partizan notions. The Jews, the Chinese, the Hindoos, the Mahomedans, the Pagans, and the Christians, through their endless sectarian divisions, are one and all strongly locally prejudiced. Each nation is locally prejudiced against all other nations — each race against all other races — each class against every other class — and, to some extent, each one against every other even in the same locality. These local prejudices prevent union and destroy charity, and, without union and charity, there can be no permanent prosperity, excellence or happiness.

Robert Owen was evidently right in regarding these large-scale emotions as the greatest obstacle to the bringing in of his utopia. But we no longer catalogue these expressions of the human spirit as prejudices. We do not view them as inferior in standing to those rational procedures which are brought into play in considered social planning. We see them as parts of the organization of human nature. These emotions are always built around values, which, though they are not all of the same worth, are the stuff out of which society is made. Social morale is always centered around values as objectives and society cannot go forward without morale.

Religion in some of its phases also deals with this kind of material. Religion is man in his believing capacity, but it is also man in his evaluating capacity and in so far as it is the latter it provides morale. Presumably religion is built around supreme values. Actually this is not always true, but at its best religion discovers, defines and defends that which is worthy of supreme devotion. A true church fosters the emotions of the people on the high plane of courage and love.

It is worth while to recognize the probability that we are entering a period which will witness another of those colossal conflicts that have taken place whenever religion struggled to substitute for the secondary values which sustained social morale its own supreme values. Such periods were those which gave birth to the Old Testament prophets and that which saw the struggle of early Christianity with emperor worship in the Roman Empire. Whenever the values posited by secular society are opposed to the values which religion declares to be supreme there results either a subordination of religion to secular society or an open conflict between the two. Whether this conflict is destructive or creative depends on circumstances. The fact is that often in the past the war between church and state has issued in the greatest thinking and willing which have ever characterized the human spirit.

It is from the vantage point of the interrelations between religion and society that we can best view the problem of human emotions in the social struggle. Society has had three classic formulas for dealing with these conflicts: (1) theocracy, (2) the totalitarian state such as the Roman Empire and its modern types, and (3) democracy. Let us consider each of them.

In a theocracy the emotions of the absolute are projected into the social order. A theocracy might be called a society in which all secular ideas are subordinated to the emotion of the absolute. God's will, as expressed in some interpretation of it, completely occupies the horizon of thought and action. It gathers up and inspires all the secondary phases of society. Such a period was that of the early church. The New Testament community was a theocracy in which religious values were supreme and men even went to the length of declaring that the family and the state were of little importance, for there was no division of labor to give these independent status. The Mormon community, in which the church is something of a totalitarian affair, owning the industries and thoroughly regimenting the lives of the people, is another illustration. The New England theocracy is a third.

Theocracies are generally defensible in their earlier

stages. They have often represented a fresh transfusion of universal-mindedness into society and inaugurated a brief period when men lived for the absolute. But sooner or later the great emotions depart and legalism comes in. The Cotton Mathers become not abettors of the people's happiness but petty legislators seeking out the minor sins of their followers. Secondary values are regimented, not inspired; petty codes crowd out the spirit. It is about this time that the youthful Benjamin Franklins arise and organize their hellfire clubs. Society once more goes secular.

In a totalitarian state the inner world of religion is subordinated to the emotions of a social order. It is not possible long to maintain a totalitarian state without a totalitarian heart. Consequently these states develop some device for regimenting the emotions of the people. Rome made its emperor the absolute. In modern times totalitarian states develop such devices as a highly emotionalized nationalism or the idea of racial purity and make this an object of supreme devotion. Of course a totalitarian society is not necessarily organized around a nation. It may center in the family or in some kind of caste system. In early days it was organized around the tribe; the individual's standing with God depended upon his membership in a tribe. But the principle is the same in all cases; some social value is set up as worthy of supreme devotion and other values are subordinated. Only the devices differ.

Totalitarianisms generally ride in on a wave of promises to act for the public good. They offer relief from some intolerable situation. The present German program came in when the German people were suffering from thirty-seven futile political parties and the almost equally futile church. There is scarcely a tyranny in the Bible which was not established benevolent-end foremost. But in time the values which have been absolutized lose their freshness and their ability to arouse emotion. They become legalistic and institutionalized, tools for oppression rather than release. Then the revolt for freedom begins.

The third formula for dealing with large-scale emotions is democracy. Democracy trusts the emotions of the people, but since the loyalties of the masses are various and center about diverse objectives democracy encounters difficulties. In a good many cases the democratic theory has been the instrument by which men have pried themselves loose from totalitarian relationships. It has emphasized revolt rather than organized relationships. The theory of democracy is that critical interplay among the various social groups and agencies is the best means of determining the standards, interwoven of the absolute and the temporary, which constitute the basis of society. Its expectation is that freedom of discussion and division of responsibility will give rise to cooperative unity. But the deplorable fact is that thus far democracies have not succeeded in achieving a free collectivism.

Democracy demands something more than separation of function but it views separation of function as prerequisite to cooperative organization of functions. It envisions an organized society which is the result of cooperative planning and working. It does not believe in the subordination of the family or the church to the state, or of the state to either. It aims at a society far more difficult to initiate and maintain than a theocracy or a totalitarian state — at a fellowship of functions in which critical interplay will ultimately give rise to a fusion of cultural values. This is the form of society which is being threatened today.

5. The Church and the Emotions of the Social Order

Different churches find themselves facing these various social orders with varying degrees of friendliness. The Roman Catholic Church in theory and practice fits in best with a theocracy. Other churches have accommodated themselves to the totalitarian society. It is in the democratic society that the Protestant church finds its natural habitat. The Protestant church does not believe in a theocracy, neither does it believe in a totalitarian state. It recognizes in the secular vocations a moral validity which the theocracy and the totalitarian state alike deny. But the problem of Protestantism lies just here, in the relationship of the church to these secular vocations. John Calvin released the latter when he declared that it was possible for men to serve God in them. The vocations however accepted liberty and rejected control. Today the Protestant churches are once more insisting that the separation between church and state, which has been a satisfactory formula for some time in the past, is no longer adequate. So far as I know no Protestant group wants to re-establish a theocracy like that of the pre-Reformation period, and it will fight to the death what it believes are the false claims of a totalitarian state. But Protestantism also affirms with equal conviction that there must be some kind of unified relationship between church and society.

The emotions which organize around the highest values are in contact and in many cases in conflict with these emotions which organize around race, nationality, class and provincial loyalties. The building of a unified society presupposes the discovery of a hierarchy of values which can be the objects of human loyalty and which will give to the inner life of man a sense of unity, wholeness and dignity.

This, it seems to me, is primarily a problem in the realm in which religion operates.   It is more fundamental than politics and statecraft; indeed it constitutes a major problem in democratic statecraft.   All our major statesmen at the present time are saying that progress in the United States awaits a change of heart, a purification of heart, on the part of the people.   If this declaration means anything at all it means that the people must turn to values which will make it possible for such plans to be formulated and such laws to be passed and executed as will lead to a better ordering of national life.

NOTES

1 Maine, *op. cit.*, p. 196.

2 Cotton Mather, *Essays to Do Good*, Dedication.

3 Richard Cabot, *The Art of Ministering to the Sick* (New York: Macmillan Co., 1936).

4 From a mimeographed document in the files of the Chicago Theological Seminary.

5 Cf. Charles A. Beard, *The Rise of American Civilization* (New York: Macmillan Co., 1927).

6 A. A. Berle and Gardiner C. Means, *The Modern Corporation and Private Property* (New York: Macmillan Co., 1933).

7 Bertrand Russell, "The Taming of Power," *Atlantic Monthly*, Oct. 1938.

The Church Nourishing the Roots of Democracy

"You people in Chicago must be very bad people," an old Hindu landlord said to me. When I asked him why he replied, "Because you kill so many cattle. Don't you know that at the root of every hair on a cow there is a god?" Then I remembered that in Hinduism the cow is a sacred animal, and the wide implications of his attitude came home to me. If anyone thinks that the agency which defines the holy does not have social importance let him try to promote good animal husbandry in a country whose religion sanctifies even the poorest of cows.

A certain strategic primacy characterizes the religious community. It can be set up and become vigorous without waiting for the perfecting of economic, social and political conditions. It is right here that religion has its opportunity. This is why it can be the leaven which leavens the whole lump. The religious community is not dependent on social conditions to such an extent that it cannot begin to exist and do its work until the environment is perfect. The minister's first obligation is to make the religious community strong and vigorous, even before he attempts to improve the political and social relationships.

The power of a religious community to project social influence depends on the vividness of its experience of God and his revelation in Christ. The church has influenced society most when it has been most preoccupied with the vital experience of God. The minister who makes the most profound social contribution is not necessarily the one who talks most about the social order, but the one who most profoundly leads his people in a successful experience of worship, which brings a consciousness both of God and of fellowship in the Kingdom of God. The religious community must be vigorous if it is to influence society.

But the religious experience cannot be held in a compartment by itself. Man's nature demands unity. Either the religious concept will influence the economic and political departments of a man's thought, or the economic and political will determine the religious. A vigorous Christianity has always projected its great ideas about God, salvation and human duty into the ordinary relationships of human living. The greatest contribution ever made to social science was made by the Hebrews in their doctrine of one God who demanded social righteousness. The Christian idea of God as Father, which grew out of Judaism, promotes both democracy and brotherliness. Democracy is more than the doctrine of self-determination, which can very easily lead to anarchy. It is the social solidarity of free men who are held together by the compulsion of love and faith.

That is why the perfecting of the worship of God as Father is a first charge on every church. Because a true idea of God is the taproot of all true social experience, it is the business of every church to lead into every community an invasion of seekers after a true experience of God. True worship gives the church an opportunity to exercise the most profound type of social ministry. In every service which binds men together in a new solidarity not manipulated from without but growing from within, the individual loses himself in a consciousness of God.

But not every service where men say " Lord, Lord! " accomplishes this purpose. Worship has the power to promote brotherhood; it has also the power to defeat brotherhood. It defeats brotherhood whenever it places undue emphasis upon form, thus causing men to exalt that which should be secondary into a place of primacy, and to make a sacred function an instrument of pride and exclusiveness. When worship does that, religion easily becomes a faction alongside of other factions. Worship defeats brotherhood when it places undue emphasis upon the individual and his experiences with God, to the neglect of his relationship to his fellow men. Evangelism so magnified the importance of inner experience that it made men introspective and neglectful of those other expressions of personal life which had to do with their obligations to those round about them.

So with prayer which forms part of the worship service. Prayer is directed toward God and not toward the congregation. Nevertheless, prayer leaders must bear in mind that all the congregations of the world are to be united in prayer to God. Liturgical churches accomplish this by careful planning of the prayers for congregational use. Nonliturgical churches can accomplish it only if the leader remembers the power of prayer, when rightly conceived, to bind the people together in a great experience of unity before the throne of God. Liturgical services are generally more effective in socializing worship and enabling men to feel their unity not only with their contemporaries but with the saints who have gone before. The Christian fellowship must always include that vaster communion of the saints.

The spoken word from the pulpit is peculiarly the channel by which the social message can be carried to the people. There is a fire which burns in the hearts of men, a passion for righteousness, which kindles ever anew the heart of the true minister. The apostolic succession in which we are all interested is the passing on of that prophetic spirit which burned in the souls of Moses and Isaiah to the succeeding generations of men who stand in the Christian pulpit and interpret the ways of God. The pulpit, after all, is the place where all the other activities of the church are interpreted. If the minister is so inclined, he can turn the whole church with all its works into " sounding brass and clanging cymbals." On the other hand, he may so define even the giving of a cup of cold water that it becomes a true social ministry.

The church exercises a prophetic ministry in all its functions if these functions are well performed. The organization of the church itself is prophetic if it gives people experience of successful associated living. For organization on the part of the church is inevitable. When trees cease to grow bark, when individuals cease to develop habits, when patriotism ceases to express itself through political parties, when culture abandons customs, then religion will cease to develop forms, creeds, social codes and organizations. Nothing is more futile than a revolt against this tendency in religion. We abandon one form only to start another.

Yet in spite of necessary mechanism the church must be a brotherhood. The cultured home is not the home devoid of organization and established ways of procedure but that in which mechanism has been reduced to a subordinate place. True culture makes mechanism the servant of neighborliness, friendship and love. The church, especially the numerous branches of the church, can become a brotherhood only by the subordination of necessary ecclesiastical mechanism to the brotherly spirit. It is the task of present-day Christianity to make the church a brotherhood, not by starting a new church, but by gaining an understanding of the old and by subordinating the " letter which killeth " to the " spirit which maketh alive."

The creation of a brotherly church involves a twofold struggle with the systems which are a necessary part of its life. First is the struggle with old systems. Tennyson said that " our little systems have their day . . . and cease to be." Everyone who has struggled with the problem of church organization knows that these little systems do not " cease to be." They are likely to hang around for a thousand years and complicate progress. Long after their usefulness has ended they claim the loyalty of stubborn devotees. The church faces a perpetual fight to free itself from the systems which it devised to meet the needs of past generations. Only a living church can hope to win that battle.

On the other hand, the church is always faced with the task of devising new systems to meet new needs. " New occasions teach new duties." New industrial orders demand new kinds of organization and new codes of action. The church which cannot project these also fails. The church should not be afraid of itemizing programs for good action. It must keep its moralizing up to date. In a word, the church succeeds, not by avoiding systems but by subordinating them to the spirit. It becomes a brotherhood, not by stripping itself of all established forms and customs and codes but by making these the servants of true brotherliness.

The coming of brotherliness into Protestantism, however, does not demand organic unity. In fact it is very easy to think of conditions under which organic unity would be an obstacle to the practice of brotherliness. For three hundred years the Protestant churches have been undergirding a fight for individual rights. If they now adopt new slogans which imply solidarity, they must not forget to leave room for a distinct freedom. Protestant solidarity will not ignore three hundred years of development in which the fight has been to find standing room for the individual.

Again, it is doubtful whether it is desirable for Protestantism so to perfect its ecclesiastical machinery that it will become oversensitive about scrapping unnecessary parts of it. The unity of Protestantism should be like that of a loose-leaf notebook, from which one can discard certain parts and to which one can add new parts without destroying the unity of the book. Protestantism will always be ragged behind and in front. In front will be those groups which desire to push ahead. Behind will be those which are lagging in the march of progress. And yet it ought to be possible for these varied groups to be conscious of their participation in a great free brotherhood whose strength is dependent on its power to give expression to a great ideal. Hence they must look upon all ecclesiastical organization as a means to an end and must apply to it the law of service which will require varied adaptations of ecclesiastical machinery in varied situations. Here too organic unity would probably hinder rather than help. Protestantism should not develop a theory which makes sacred what must always be secondary and which can justify itself only on the basis of its ability to serve something higher.

Society is sick from an overdose of materialism and of provincial loyalties. Paul was perfectly right when he said, " The mind of the flesh is death." Out of the untempered loyalty to race, class and nation — the ultimate reality for many people — come " enmities, strife, jealousies, wrath, factions and divisions." The hatreds of the world are cumulative. A society based on force and fear will always disintegrate through its own self-generated hatred. Our deepest maladies are moral and spiritual. Only a sense of a reality which stands over against the natural world, and which is of such infinite value that it makes the lesser goals of human striving seem small in comparison, will dispel the fevers which annoy the souls of modern men. The church must offer to men the opportunity to enter into this realm, which is open to the " pure in heart " and to those " who hunger and thirst after righteousness."

In the place of the religious fraternity which Jesus launched stands the modern church. Can the modern church be a brotherhood? From the social standpoint, all other questions are secondary. Can the modern church achieve a group-consciousness which arises to something of universality? If it is to do so, it must become more to men than their consciousness of nationality, class, race and provincial locality. It will see in the strife and hatred between classes, races and nations an essential defeat of its own desire for a growing friendship between men of Christian profession of every race, class and nation.

No greater offense against a brotherly church can be committed than to allow the church to fall a victim to factions and itself become a faction alongside other factions. It may be said that in its social ministry the church will to a great extent stand or fall by its ability to lift its people to a place where friendship transcends national, racial and class divisions. Not until members of the Christian church feel a bond of unity which cannot be disrupted by slogans of nationalism and class prejudice, will the church have made its greatest contribution to social living.

It is not possible to make into a church a body of people who do not like one another. A Christian brotherhood, however, is not a social club. A group of nice people who like one another and who meet and enjoy fellowship to-gether fall short of that which Jesus intended the church to be. The friendships of the church must not be selfish. It is here that the church finds itself in danger of being im-paled on one of the horns of a dilemma. It can, on the one hand, ignore the natural groupings of men and women, and devote itself entirely to being a universal fellowship which knows neither bond nor free, neither Jew nor Gen-tile. The danger in this case is that it will fail to reach both the bond and the free, both the Jew and the Gentile. The church must remember that the apostle who coined that phrase considered that he himself was specially or-dained to the Gentiles and shaped his ministry to that end. On the other hand, there is danger that the church, in adapting itself to the congenial groupings of men and women, will fall a victim to these natural tendencies and will cease to be a universal fellowship.

The part of wisdom for the church is to recognize the need of both courses of action. It must organize churches which take account of the natural tendencies of various groups — tendencies shaped by the ways in which they make their living, by national conditions and by race and training. Having made this concession, it must strive with all its might to carry out its gospel of reconciliation, which will make all men one in the fellowship and calling committed to them by Jesus Christ. Creativeness is of the essence of Christian fellowship. It seeks always to extend itself into new fields. It is happiest when it is bridging gaps. Its sweetest moments are those at which it rises in new discoveries into the richness of universal friendship. Its very laws spring from the sense of fellowship.

Right in the early Christian community was not a legal code but what a group of men sitting about a fellowship table decided to be the law of love in their relationships. In this face-to-face conference there was accomplished a real reconciliation and a bridging of the gaps which often separate human beings. Here master and slave found a unity which tempered the relationship and robbed it of its harshness, and ultimately led to a change in the status of the slave. All this is a part of the philosophy of friendship by which Christianity would solve the problems of the social order.

The giving and the breaking of fellowship brings a most serious crisis in the church. When Jesus extends fellowship to the woman at the well, something real and fundamental is happening in Jewish society. A historic chasm is bridged by this act. The breaking of fellowship is just as serious, though its social consequences have generally been taken too lightly. When the Methodist Church of America broke fellowship over the slavery issue, Henry Clay was moved to write:

Scarcely any public occurrence has happened for a long time that gave me so much real concern and pain as the menaced separation of the church by a line throwing all the free states on one side and all the slave states on the other.

I will not say that such a separation would necessarily produce a dissolution of the political union of these states; but the example would be fraught with imminent danger and, in cooperation with other causes, unfortunately existing, its tendency on the stability of the confederacy would be perilous and alarming.

Entertaining these views, it would afford me the highest satisfaction to hear of an adjustment of the controversy, a reconciliation between the opposing parties in the church and the preservation of its unity.

The break came because the church was under obligation to seek fellowship with the Negro as well as with the white man and could not do so while it acquiesced in the Negro's slavery. The fellowship which the church seeks to realize is not an easygoing affair. It is not to be easily given; neither is it to be easily broken. It may be broken only in the interest of moral progress and with the aim of ultimate good to the one to whom it is denied. It must be given, not on the basis of race or class, but on the basis of character. Christians must be slow to anger and quick to forgive. If the church draws a line, it must be a line which defines real moral boundaries and on the church's side there must remain a yearning for the ultimate restoration of unbroken communion. The real indictment against the divisions of Christendom is that they have ceased to have moral significance, that they distort the Christian conscience rather than clarify it. The church can win the confidence of all men only by standing for justice for all. When it permits special privilege for any, it forfeits the respect of all.

Is this idea of the church as the force which above all is able to improve social conditions a valid one? Is the relation of the Christian fellowship to society such as I have outlined? There are four answers to that question which it is worth while to note once more in passing. First of all, there are those who say that the whole constellation of religious ideas represents an attempt on the part of thwarted humanity to grasp some kind of visionary satisfaction out of life. Communism will tell you that anybody who holds those ideas is trying to compensate himself for his inadequacies in real living. He is building up a picture of an unreal world because he does not have the stuff to go out and live in the real world.

Second, there are those who recognize the validity of the concept of fellowship but maintain that it belongs in the monastery. This is the formula of the Roman Catholic Church, but even among Protestants one encounters groups who argue for the little islands of brotherhood which can be established and safeguarded though the big catastrophe should come.

Third, there are those who declare that brotherhood can be exercised only in the primary relationships of life, and that we but invite disappointment when we try to extend it into the public order. "You ministers," these people would say, "can go out and talk about those ideas so long as you talk about the family and the neighborhood, because there those ideas can be realized, there you can have social cohesion based on trust and confidence, there you can have a philosophy of mutual aid. But you would be very wise not to advance beyond that because the moment you do you are simply inviting futility."

But there is a fourth answer to this question. A Christianity that hides in monasteries or is held within the confines of family and neighborhood is a meager kind of religion. The Christian constants and the sense of responsibility they foster need all of life for their field. There is an inevitable relationship between them and the social order — a relationship not unlike a fellowship of architects who are building a temple and find their fellowship in mutual stimulation to good works.

Modern science has given us a world-wide community which to a great degree is operating on the basis of laws opposed to Christian ethics and is gradually destroying the few Christian principles that are still observed in the face-to-face relationship. The result is a society that, both in its national and in its universal aspects, is not only pagan but is so filled with conflicts that it looks as though it were going to be self-destructive. If we are going to try to do our Christian duty as responsible people, we will have to seek to capture for Christian ethics the world of secondary relationships, business and politics. This is a twofold problem, that of recovering a belief and that of extending the experience we have gained in the family and the neighborhood.

The doctrine of Christian love is something which roots in our gospel, something that is comprehensible, something that is experimental. Now that we have recovered love as basic in our consciousness, we face the problem of creating communities in which Christian responsibility can be exercised. You just cannot take your Christian responsibility out into modern society as it now is. Society simply makes a martyr of you. There is no ultimate logic in playing forever the role of a martyr — not if you can create communities in which it is possible to exercise Christian responsibility.

When the Christian churches of the world met at Oxford for their conference in 1937, they chose as their slogan, " Let the church be the church." As it stands that slogan may mean almost anything. In order to be useful it needs amplification at two points.

First, it needs to be clearly recognized that the church cannot be the church in a society which does not permit freedom of worship and freedom of organization, and that it is the business of the church to create such a society. For if the church does not create such a society it will not be created at all. If the church ignores this obligation it is likely to be awakened to it when it is too late. It is an interesting fact that none of the Calvinistic countries in which it was considered good religion to cause trouble for the political state is now trying to regiment the church, while those countries in which the church either allowed God to take care of the political order or claimed the right to control the political order, are now attempting to regiment the church or to throw it out altogether.

Second, the slogan " Let the church be the church " does not define the church. It is necessary to evaluate critically the *kind* of church which is under consideration. This is especially important today in view of the many attempts to move from the present divided state of Christendom to a church universal in one form or other. Here we can learn a lesson from the attempt to unite the nations of the world in the League of Nations. At the close of the World War, Woodrow Wilson and his fellow enthusiasts sought to create a world political society. In their enthusiasm they forgot that only purified nations could be fit members of a league of peace, and they sought to join together nations which were international implements for exploiting the weak peoples of the earth. What was buried behind the idealistic façade of the League of Nations sent up an unsavory odor to high heaven before the ink was dry on all the signatures to its covenant. The league was lax in restraining aggressor nations because all its member nations were products and practitioners of aggression.

In their anxiety to establish an organic Christendom the advocates of a universal church are in danger of falling into the same error. They offer membership to groups which have been the advocates of the closed mind and the religious work departments of empire capitalism, and are today monuments of ecclesiastical egotism multiplying jobs for clergymen and maintaining them in comparative opulence. A united church which throws the symbols of universality over such groups will be consigned to the Valley of Gehenna for the same reason that other social refuse was sent there. The problem that faces the new Holy Catholic Church is that of finding instruments of self-criticism which will work as effectively as did the old competitive system. That system, with all its faults, at least allowed the critics of the church to start a new church.

Is the church strong enough and wise enough to create the new society which alone will save civilization? It would be unrealistic to deny the fact that the church itself frequently behaves badly. It does so because it shares in the social order to such an extent that in many of its phases it is very much like the social order. The social order — and that includes the industrial order — often determines the nature of the churches which exist in it. The churches of Chicago are an excellent example of the way religions drift into a community. They are the result of four great racial migrations to the city.

The first migration was that of the period from 1830 to
1860. Most of the immigrants came from the eastern seacoast or from the British Isles. This period planted the
Methodist, Presbyterian, Episcopal, Baptist and Roman
Catholic churches in the city. The second period, about
1860 to 1890, was marked by heavy migrations from north
continental Europe. With these migrations came the
great Lutheran churches and the north European Roman
Catholic churches. The third period, beginning about
1890 and continuing to 1914, witnessed the migration
from southern Europe which brought great Catholic increase. The Polish and Italian Catholic churches grew to
as high as twenty thousand members each. With the coming of the World War and the shutting off of European migration, labor began to drift in from the south and from the
farms of the adjacent states and Chicago entered a period
of Protestant growth with large accessions of Negroes to
the Methodist and Baptist denominations. On the basis
of these facts it is fair to say that Chicago's churches have
been planted by the labor policies of the great industries;
not denominational secretaries but the needs of business
have distributed the churches in the city.

It would be an exaggeration to say that these churches,
immediately upon their arrival in Chicago, began to teach
and train a public-minded citizenship. The extreme mobility of urban population has kept all the churches guess-
ing about the problems which have to do with self-preservation. They have been happy if the vertical and
horizontal mobility of the city has not completely torn
them to pieces. Only the Roman Catholic Church has followed a well planned parish system. The others have
lived by a catch-as-catch-can system which works to the ad-

vantage of those who are at the receiving end of the population shift, and to the great disadvantage of those who see their membership departing to suburban areas.

The second factor that has determined the behavior of the churches is their attitude toward society. It is not in accordance with the genius of all the churches to think in terms which can be characterized as public-minded. There are among American churches at least four easily recognized groupings based on their social theories.

First is what may be called the apocalyptic group. Their social point of view is similar to that of the New Testament community, which anticipated an early divine intervention in the social order. They " dynamited " the prevailing order with the doctrine of the second coming of Christ. The fact that that order was evil brought them more consolation than anguish, for the pervasiveness of evil made them certain that Christ's coming was near at hand. This point of view prevails today in a surprisingly large section of the American churches. They have little interest in improving the social order, and do not bring any great pressure to bear on the state or on other social institutions.

The second group reflects the historic point of view of the Lutheran church, which accepts the existing state as a God-given order, one which the church is not called upon either to improve or to disapprove of publicly. The American churches of Lutheran persuasion have been very loth to participate in any movement which would seem to go beyond this point of view.

The third group shares the theory held originally by the Calvinistic churches — that it is good religion to cause trouble for the political state. This American churches of the Calvinistic school have not failed to do. They have acted on the belief that their religious commitments oblige them to participate in political life.

The fourth group is a clearly defined one — that of the Roman Catholic churches. The Roman Church has not departed from the point of view of the Middle Ages; it still believes that the state should be subordinated to the church, although it has for some time shown a tendency to define the state as a separate entity and betrayed an unwillingness to see that duty to church and duty to state may conflict.

But more important than the churches' lack of interest in public questions has been their lack of discernment when they have participated. The record of the behavior of metropolitan clergy with reference to civic and political issues is neither all black nor all white. But unfortunately black predominates. The fine work of a Parkhurst, a Gladden and a Graham Taylor does not outweigh the mischief done by the great body of the clergy. Their record is sad enough to keep their successors humble for a thousand years. In most of the great political conflicts of America the clergy took the side of privilege. They were utterly unable to discern the significance of such men as Thomas Jefferson, Andrew Jackson and William Jennings Bryan, much less to interpret it fairly. At the time of the Hamilton-Jefferson conflict, the record shows, almost all clergymen championed the Federalist cause. Claude Bowers says of this period that

. . . all over New England and in New York and Philadelphia, ministers were preaching politics with an intemperance of denunciation and a recklessness of truth that seems incredible today. The game of the politicians to picture Jefferson as an atheist, a scoffer at religion who despised the church and laughed at the Bible, was entrusted to the ministerial corps, which did the best it could! . . . In Connecticut these ministers were the backbone of the Federalist party machine, with Dwight as their leader, than whom none more offensively intolerant ever breathed curses on a foe. In Massachusetts when the Rev. Ebenezer Bradford espoused the cause of democracy, he was ferociously abused by his fellow ministers and the Federalist papers, ostracized in the name of Christ by his fellow clergymen and refused a pulpit in Essex county. It was not a time when ministers in some sections were making much of the action of Christ in seeking his disciples among workers and fishermen.[1]

At the time of the controversy between Jackson and Adams the clergy again took sides with the reactionaries. Jackson's opponents had the support not only of the metropolitan newspapers, the Federal office-holders, manufacturers and bankers, but also of the great majority of clergymen. And so in many another political battle. Clerical forces almost invariably identified themselves with reaction.

The record for the great struggle of the 1890's between the capitalists of the Gilded Age and the radical Democrats is unusually complete. Mark Hanna, the leader of the Republican capitalists, was able to line up the metropolitan clergy almost to a man. It was the old issue between those who had borrowed money when wheat was worth a dollar a bushel and those who were trying to collect the debts in full when wheat had dropped to forty cents a bushel — an issue which is so easy to solve by declaring that people should pay their honest debts. The suggestion of Bryan and Altgeld that it would be fair to inflate the currency by coinage of silver met with violent opposition from those whom Hanna represented. Organized labor joined in the cry against Bryan because it saw in free silver a threat to the buying power of wages. In the eastern centers of commerce, Hanna's point of view had the support of men like Parkhurst, MacArthur, Henry Van Dyke, W. H. Faunce, Charles H. Thompson and others equally notable. In Chicago, the meeting place of east and west, the clergy let itself go. During the last week of September and October in 1896, Chicago's newspapers were filled with reports of sermons in which Bryan was called all the varieties of demagogue which the amenities of pulpit language would allow. Here are typical excerpts taken from the reports of sermons which appeared in a single newspaper on a single Monday morning in September of that hectic campaign:

But now has arisen another sectional prejudice, being strengthened by him who is going over our country speaking of one large and important section of these United States as the " enemies' country." These are not the words of a patriot or a safe popular leader, but rather of a demagogue. No less regrettable is the effort on his part to array what he is pleased to call " the masses against the classes."

The other impending evil, in some respects the greatest of all, is that of a depreciated and uncertain currency with the consequent dishonor that would attach to the nation and all who desire it that they may earlier pay their debts. . . . Thank God, as in 1776 and as was true in the north in 1861, so now the ministry, with almost complete unanimity, see eye to eye in this crisis.[2] — *Rev. J. W. Caldwell, Park Avenue Methodist Church.*

Now the question we have to answer is whether the proposition to open our mints to the free and unlimited coinage of silver at the ratio of 16 to 1 will give this country a depreciated currency. If that can be shown we are face to face with an issue which should rouse every American citizen who has at his heart his country's honor and his country's welfare to a sense of the responsibility of citizenship.[3] — *Rev. Dr. Rubinkam, University Congregational Church.*

The critical stage in the progress of disease is no time to test the quality of certain individual remedies. We should not work and pray for the realization of an impossible or experimental platform of political principles but a possible and conservative one.[4] — *Rev. J. P. Brushingham, Fulton Street Methodist Episcopal Church.*

Confessedly the amassing of wealth means thrift, ingenuity, economy and perseverance for the individual, while at the same time it ministers to great treasure to home and market place. Savagery always means poverty. When barbarism starts toward intelligence and Christianity it starts toward wealth.[5] — *Rev. Newell Dwight Hillis, Central Music Hall.*

The demagogue is a spectacular candidate, appealing to ignorance and the meanest motives. He makes an ambitious display of his love for the plain people.[6] — *Rev. J. Q. A. Henry, LaSalle Avenue Baptist Church.*

The overwhelming majority of our churches' constituency consists of the common people and if, in the matter of the issues involved in the present presidential contest, the Christian churches and Christian ministers are almost unanimously arrayed upon one side it is not because they have been bribed or browbeaten by plutocrats, but because they love their fellow toilers so well they want to see honest labor paid in honest money.[7] — *Rev. P. S. Henson, First Baptist Church.*

Dr. W. H. Thomas of the People's Church was a solitary exception. He gave more tolerant interpretation of the

rising tide of popular feeling against the forces which
Mark Hanna represented. In the course of his sermon he
said:

There is a wide feeling that the wealth and power of the
country are coming into the hands of a few, that money powers are oppressing the people through the monopolies and
trusts, that laboring people and the poor have not a fair chance
in the struggle of life. If this is true it is a sad truth. God is
on the side of the people, the side of humanity, and our country should be on the side of God.[8]

Since the beginning of this century there has been a
change of attitude among large sections of the American
clergy. Seminaries today give training in economics and
sociology, and the social gospel is gaining more and more
adherents. But it is undeniable that the clergy as a whole
still tends toward provincialism, and that the church as
an institution is still conservative. That this is so is not
a matter of chance. I can give five good reasons why the
church will not lead a crusade.

1. The church must deal with old people, but the word
of the crusader is, " Let the dead bury their dead."

2. The church must deal with children, but the word of
the crusader is, " Woe to those who give suck in that time."

3. The church carries a heavy burden of benevolence
and those who carry such burdens must stay close to those
who have the means to be benevolent.

4. The church is a cross section of society and society
does not crusade majority-end foremost.

5. The church can always get a majority to vote for old
causes, but new causes divide its members. Moreover,
when economic crises come there will always be someone

to drag the red herring of religious prejudice or drink regulation across the road and thus the church will lose the
trail of a great social wrong.

⚬⚬⚬

But beside these causes for the churches' conservatism
stands the fact that when they undertake to lead a crusade
they tend to forget their function. The churches behave
badly when they try to be the community instead of the
interpreter of the community. There is a difference between symbol and substance. Let me illustrate. Some
time ago I heard the story of a social worker who called every Monday morning on an Italian family with eight children and always took with her a little glass of jelly. Now
a glass of jelly, from the standpoint of substance, would not
go far in that family of ten, but as a symbol that glass of
jelly was very important. It was a contribution toward
the interpretation of personal relationships and as such
was far more significant than a contribution to the family's
food supply. Not to know the difference between symbol
and substance, in so far as church work is concerned, seems
to me a grave failing.

Recently William Frazier, in an article in *Advance*,[9] rid-
iculed the theory that the church, to be important, had to
be useful in the sense of doing something. I thought his
point was in general very well taken. He tells of an experience which befell him at the time of the Connecticut
river flood, during which some of the people whose houses
had been wrecked lived in the church building. He heard
one man remark, " Well, I am glad to see the church doing
something useful at last." Frazier has rather a good time
satirizing the people who found it necessary, in order to

justify the church, to plead that it was making a contribution to the housing facilities of persons in need.

It is, I think, partly this desire to have something happen which leads us astray. The Mormon Church recently decided to take all its people off relief and to become the sole agent in Utah for the distribution of charity to Mormons. The newspapers have given a great deal of space to this matter and there has been much praise of it. One of my students has just completed a study of this subject. This shows that despite the fact that the Mormon Church can administer charity within the ranks of its own people without pauperizing them, a number of very serious problems arise. The church becomes cluttered up with the administrative problems involved in giving relief to many thousands of people — a task so enormous that it looks as though the church itself may be bogged down by it. Moreover, relief administration on the part of the church drives something of a wedge through the community because not all people in any Utah community are Mormons, and a good many of the more or less negligent Mormons are not getting their share of relief. This situation has come about because it is the theory of the Mormon Church that it *is* the community rather than the inspirer of the community.

Again, the church easily confuses the progress of the Kingdom with ecclesiastical success. The multiplication of church buildings, the increase in the number of preachers and prelates, the swelling of ecclesiastical bank accounts are taken as indications that the influence of the church is spreading. At the time when the Roman Catholic Church had reached the zenith of her power in that country, the Archbishop of Mexico was a fitting symbol of the institution he represented. I came across this description of that prelate in Mme. Calderon de la Barca's classic *Life in Mexico* written, I think, in 1837:

. . . Were I to choose a situation here it would undoubtedly be that of the Archbishop of Mexico, the most enviable in the world to those who would enjoy a life of tranquillity, ease and universal adoration. He is a pope without the trouble, or a tenth part of the responsibility. He is venerated more than the Holy Father is in enlightened Rome and, like kings in the good old times, can do no wrong. His salary amounts to about one hundred thousand dollars, and a revenue might be made by the sweetmeats alone which are sent him from all the nuns in the republic.

His palace in town, his well cushioned carriage, well conditioned horses, and sleek mules, seem the very perfection of comfort. In fact, comfort, which is unknown amongst the profane of Mexico, has taken refuge with the archbishop; and though many drops of it are shed on the shaven heads of all bishops, curates, confessors and friars, still in his illustrious person it concentrates as in a focus.

He, himself, is a benevolent, good-hearted, good-natured, portly and jovial personage, with the most *laissez-aller* air and expression conceivable. He looks like one on whom the good things of this world have fallen in a constant and benignant shower, which shower hath fallen on a rich and fertile soil. He is generally to be seen leaning back in his carriage, dressed in purple, with amethyst cross, and giving his benediction to the people he passes. He seems engaged in a pleasant revery, and his countenance wears an air of the most placid and insouciant content. He enjoys a good dinner, good wine, and ladies' society, but just sufficiently to make his leisure hours pass pleasantly, without indigestion from the first, headaches from the second, or heartaches from the third.

So does his life seem to pass on like a deep, untroubled stream, on whose margin grow sweet flowers, on whose waters the bending trees are reflected, but on whose placid face no lasting impression is made.[10]

It required a successful institution to support a prelate in that style. But the success was of a kind the church can well do without. The lot of the mass of Mexicans in the days when the archbishop rode softly through the streets was worse than that of the coolies in the China of today.

There is no doubt that on many occasions in the past the church has behaved badly. But after all her sins and mistakes have been counted up, the fact remains that the stream of life which flows through the church from the foot of the cross is the purest stream that flows through history. If all the churches were abolished we would not get rid of religion. In the place of the present manifestations of religion there would arise soothsayers, clairvoyants, necromancers, ouija-board experts, astrologers and palm readers. There would be multiplication of all those devices by which the unaided human spirit seeks to answer for itself the great questions of life which have to do with ultimate self-definition and self-direction. No law-abiding social order could be built out of people who assume as the major thesis of their thinking that the universe is petulant and freakish in its central economy.

The validity of the Christian church's claim to be the nourishing home of spiritual responsibility lies in its right to hold up for human worship a person who establishes roles, determines behavior and defines causes worthy to be the causes of a universal society. The validity of the Chris-

tian church's claim to be the nourishing fellowship of creative living roots in the way it approaches humanity with
its messages. Not all the church's approaches become the
basis for creative living on the part of those who are its
members. If the church comes to you with a code, it does
not become for you the home of spiritual maturity; if it
comes to you with a law, it does not become the nourisher
of creative living; if it comes to you with a book or an institution, it does not become for you a community of the
spirit; but if it comes to you with a vocation, a call, a role,
if you will, which has its source in Jesus Christ, even
though it is an institution, even though it has a book and
a multitude of codes — it becomes for you the fellowship
of creative living.

The function of the Christian church is to maintain in
contemporary society the passion of a redeeming God.
The church has the conviction that its task is to carry on
in the world what God was doing in Jesus. To be sure, it
must hold this conviction with certain acknowledged reservations. It must know that it has no monopoly on God's
revelation in the world. It must recognize that again and
again God has used some instrument other than the church
for the revelation of his will for humanity. On occasion
revolutions have come along to teach the church lessons
which were greatly overdue. Again, the church shares
with other institutions a total ministry to humanity. It
must recognize the validity of family, school, neighborhood, business and the state as sharers in the total program
of human well-being. It must trust these institutions as
well as criticize them. It must be a learning church and
accept criticism from them, for only a learning church can
be a teaching church.

But recognition of all these reservations does not militate against the conviction that it is possible for the church to keep alive in human society the passion which was once resident only in the person of its Founder. The sole task of the Christian church is to keep vivid in the world the person Jesus Christ as the role-creating person in a Christian fellowship. The social message of a church does not begin when the church meets society; it begins where man meets brother man and God meets both in worship. The church carries a social message in worship and in social action.

NOTES

[1] Claude Bowers, *Jefferson and Hamilton* (New York: Houghton Mifflin Co., 1926), p. 473.

[2] *Chicago Times-Herald*, Sept. 15, 1896.

[3] *Ibid.*

[4] *Ibid.*

[5] *Ibid.*

[6] *Ibid.*

[7] *Ibid.*

[8] *Ibid.*

[9] William Frazier, " Something Practical," *Advance*, Oct. 1937.

[10] Mme. Calderon de la Barca, *Life in Mexico* (Everyman's ed.), pp. 218–19.

The Church in Social Education and Social Action

Spiritual maturity and ethical awareness in individuals and groups are the first necessity of democracy. Can we educate for these qualities? The little red schoolhouse answered the needs of a pioneer society which lived face to face and learned democracy in its daily living. But the society of today is vastly complex and specialized in all its parts. Can we educate for associated living in a democracy of a hundred and twenty million people?

Training for democracy is not a mechanical matter. A system of education which makes dependents of men and expects of them only obedience to law and custom cannot produce democratic individuals. Neither can a system which inflates men's egotism. The school for democracy aims to produce an individual who is aware of the fact that he is not self-made but has received more than he can give, an individual trained in social judgment, courageous to challenge old systems and rise in rebellion against ancient tyrannies.

Thus far our educational system has not produced individuals of that kind. The indictment against it is severe. It has not consciously trained for brotherhood but has allowed conduct to root in some form of individualism. It has made of its subjects skillful performers of petty chores rather than men of moral judgment and action. It has been content to teach the skills and techniques of living, but has not concerned itself with the goals. In attempting to provide a basis for ethical conduct it has stressed the motives of fear rather than the motives naturally implied in the conception of God as a Father who calls upon men to be brothers.

Nor has its training given a clear vision of the goals of conduct which would make its students free builders in the realm of righteousness. The builder of a house can set to work freely only if he has a mental image of the house he wishes to construct, understands the laws of architecture and has a knowledge of building materials. Our democracy has neglected to pay the price of educating its members for great social action. Yet only as it faithfully sets forth the goals of conduct and in alliance with science gives a knowledge of principles and materials can it produce free workmen for a better social order.

Can we transform our system so that it will educate not primarily to increase man's skill in developing himself and his material environment, but in a way which will create responsible living in terms of an associated world? What is involved in such education?

In India there is a school called the School for Princes, where those are educated who are born to rulership. I have sometimes wondered what one would put into the curriculum of a school for princes — something, surely, that would have to do with the sense of vocation. A good deal in the way of techniques and skills would be included but the ultimate object would undoubtedly be to give the student a sense of his calling, to build his consciousness of vocation so that he would know what it is to feel and act like a prince.

The old Hebrew synagogue was, among other things, a

place for the building of the consciousness of being a good Hebrew. It really was a great folk school. Its curriculum was made up largely of the materials which have gone into the Old Testament, the tales of Judaism's heroes, its great patriarchs and prophets, leaders and kings. This was the stuff with which teachers in Israel fed the minds of the on-coming generations of young Hebrews. We of today enjoy reading those heroic tales, and we can imagine somewhat their effect on the minds of youths who identified themselves with the group from which these great ones had sprung. There were the stories of the relations of the Hebrews with their God in the past and the accounts of many a contest in the long struggle for righteousness. There were the great songs which commemorated the various experiences that befell the Hebrews on their age-long march toward the Promised Land. There was the story of Nehemiah rebuilding the old home community. No community-building story in the world is equal to that tale of the rescue of the community from disintegration. Exodus in its latter part or Deuteronomy would be an excellent textbook for a course in neighborhood responsibility. They show graphically how ordinary neighborhood problems piled up and how they were handled with more or less of a sense of justice. They present cases in terms of neighborhood justice — what to do if the neighbor's ox comes into the pasture, if there is a fire in the wheatfield, if somebody breaks in and steals.

But the folk school has its limitations. Apparently Mr. Hitler doesn't know that, but it is true. It creates race consciousness, and in the end a school that creates only race consciousness is calamitous. In time the Hebrew school for responsible living ceased to be a folk school and with the emergence of the New Testament moved out into something of universal significance.

The folk schools established by Bishop Grundtvig in Denmark resembled the Hebrew synagogue in some respects. In those schools only those were allowed to teach who could speak the " living word." Just what Grundtvig meant by the " living word " has never become quite clear to me. I think he meant a " word," a method that enlarged the individual's sense of his life's importance in a vocation and which communicated the sense of mission to other people. At any rate, the bishop's schools did not give degrees; they did not have much to do with techniques such as reading, writing and arithmetic. They were schools which fed the student's sense of vocation, of being a citizen of Denmark and a sharer in his country's traditions. He was made familiar with the great Danish myths and tales. He gathered together with his fellows to sing songs, read inspirational literature and think through his nation's problems. Grundtvig's personal slogan became the slogan of the Danish people: " That which I have lost outwardly I will win inwardly." I was in Denmark at the time England was threatening to close her markets to Danish bacon and dairy products. That would have been a severe blow to Danish prosperity. I asked a Danish acquaintance of mine what they were going to do about it. " Well," he said, " Denmark has always been able to live by improving the quality of what she does." That slogan of Grundtvig's still holds good.

The United States can learn a lesson from these schools. True, our problem is a little different. Most of our people do not need to have their self-confidence restored. As I know them, Americans are amply fortified at that point. But we face nothing less than the nation-wide breakdown of a sense of responsible living. We need schools that will develop a sense of responsibility in a world of human beings whose only future lies in an achieved brotherliness. Just as the ancient Hebrew synagogue trained men in the vocation of being Hebrews and the Danish folk school trained men in the vocation of being citizens of Denmark, so the schools of America must train men in the vocation of being responsible members of a democratic society. They must foster that sense of divine love which is more powerful than all those degenerating forces which drag man down to the level of selfishness — the desire to hate, the desire to be a member of a particular racial group, the blind enthusiasms of patriotism.

Responsible living can be generated only in central institutions for the training of the will along these lines. And this is a matter our public education has been absolutely unwilling to deal with. It has refused even to consider the question of the perversion or perfection of the human will, or at most it has answered it by references to the virtues of patriotism or to some kind of self-development. The whole realm of the training of youth has been invaded by pagan ideas which cannot stand up under the stress and strain of life. We see the result — a generation of young people who fall victims to any major drive they encounter, because their will is organized around some short-time objective like business success or sex desire or class-consciousness or patriotism.

The time has come for the launching in the United States of an educational program which frankly states:

" We are out to educate for responsible living in the modern world." Fragmentary efforts in that direction are already under way and have clarified the principles which must underlie such a program.

The school for responsible living will frankly expect its pupils to take part in the relationships of family, neighborhood and community life. The trouble with many colleges and schools is that they uproot young people from the field of all their natural responsibilities, organize them in such a community of subsidized irresponsibility as the modern campus, and nevertheless expect them to develop a will for responsible conduct. As De Tocqueville implied, the sense of responsibility is generated in the local community; and on the basis of the local community one is able to comprehend the great community.

The school for responsible living will emphasize not science but duty, loyalty, faith, belief and courage for social adventuring. It will ally itself with all the vigorous expressions in the community of the will to live on a cooperative basis. It will be a Christian thought center for a new America. Its constitution will declare that it is dedicated to a more just and Christian order in terms of the various relationships which I have mentioned. The troubled times through which we are passing give witness to the fact that the evils of modern society are disasters of the heart and not of the head. Once more we are able to appreciate the saying: " Keep thy heart with all diligence for out of it come all the issues of life."

So much for the principles of the school for democracy. What would its curriculum include? Very much the kind of material the ancient Hebrew synagogue used, the kind Grundtvig used, all the great literature which deals with loyalty and duty and love. That material would be presented in such a way as to create world consciousness rather than national or racial consciousness. It would teach people to say " ought " once more. " Ought " is a word that has dropped out of the American vocabulary and in other countries has been vitiated. I have a friend who is a very eminent teacher in a very eminent university. He says to the students in his seminar: " When you come into this seminar you must part with the word ' ought ' at the door. It is not to be brought in. Here we are analyzing, here we are taking the objective attitude." The application of that objective attitude to all situations has brought trouble to our universities and to our whole democratic society, especially today when they encounter a totalitarian state whose people are perfectly willing to say " ought " in terms of race and nationality. The objective attitude cannot stand up against the national " ought." Democracy must develop its own type of " ought," one that is more vigorous, more universal, more discerning and more confident because it is more deeply rooted and because it is for a larger welfare.

The school for democracy would study immediate problems as a step to universal problems. It would not at first allow its pupils to deal with universal problems, for there is danger in that, the danger of a kind of otherworldliness which has nothing to do with heaven and eternal life but consists in conscientiousness about the remote. It ignores the evils at the door to protest against the evils in far places. It leads the American to forget the plight of the Negro in the United States and lament the fate of Ethiopia. Responsible living, however, begins with oneself and one's neighbor. Concrete dealing with the problems of one's own community leads gradually to concrete dealing with the problems of the world community.

To sum up: The school for democracy will train its pupils to interpret life and to play responsibly their roles in society. It will assign to each individual his task in the building of the general welfare. It will take the great motives which come welling up out of Christianity and direct them into the channels of public-mindedness.

There was a time when the churches of this country directly accepted their responsibility for education of this sort. There was a time when they bore half the burden of higher education. But some of the institutions founded by the denominations have been taken over by the state and the others have simply duplicated secular education. They have been forced to do so because their graduates want to get jobs. Nowadays church colleges are doing approximately what state schools are doing: training people in the skills of life.

Secular patterns have invaded even our Sunday schools. There are probably eighteen million people in the Sunday schools, almost as many as in the secular schools. But the Sunday school does not take itself seriously in this matter of responsible living. It has not known exactly what it was trying to do. There was a period when the Sunday school attempted to prove that it was like secular education. Then it slipped over into slogans of self-development. Sometimes it has taught the Scriptures, sometimes it has taught projects, and a great deal of the time it has taught nothing at all.

Consider organizations like the Y.M.C.A. or the Y.W.

C.A. These represent a significant attempt on the part of the churches to come out into the field with a new type of education. But in general they have become agencies for training of the body or training in personal efficiency. Neither is dealing with the pressing problems of life.

If our church institutions can be brought to focus their attention once more on the true aims of education I can see a place for almost all of them. A large number of the church-founded colleges — small liberal arts institutions — which are about to wink out, can be salvaged in this way. Reorientation of this kind would aid also the work that is being done in the Sunday school. Our young people's conferences, with their missionary and social education, are just on the edge of it. There has been an enormous growth in young people's conferences all over the country. They have developed a great missionary literature for building the mind on an international scale. There are signs on the horizon, it seems to me, of a distinct advance in that field, the biggest unoccupied field in American education at the present time. It is the task of the churches to push forward.

But if the church is to help in the building of communities wherein people can be responsible it must work in another field also. It must constantly criticize society and all the institutions of society, and give expression to that criticism in action.

The right of the church to do these things has often been challenged, though perhaps never so violently as today. For today the economic conflict is, at least as viewed from the outside, the central one, and the economic war is being

waged with peculiar bitterness.   Hence many of the
church's criticisms are directed against the prevailing economic setup, which all too often frustrates the individual
in his search for the abundant life.   Let me relate an experience of mine which seems to illustrate all the issues
involved in social action on the part of the church.

A number of years ago there came to my morning class
several students who were pastors of churches located
northwest of Chicago in the milkshed.   They reported that
the farmers were rioting over the new campaigns on the
part of the city and the national government to eliminate
tuberculosis from the cattle which supplied Chicago's milk.
The governmental forces were driving the campaign
through ruthlessly, and the farmers could only stand help-
lessly by and witness the destruction of the herds they had
built up over periods of twenty-five years or more.   The
ministers were much concerned, since neighborhood rioting and hatred of the farmers for the city seemed to be destroying all sense of fellowship and Christian charity.   My
department sent Carl Hutchinson out to establish first-
hand contact with the situation.   Aided by the Federal
Council of Churches, he carried on a study which was eventually published and had considerable influence in estab-
lishing what became the largest farmers' organizing and
marketing agency in the United States.

In the midst of the controversy a prominent churchman
of Chicago telephoned me and said that in his opinion
this situation was entirely outside the province of a theological seminary.   A little later he sent me the following
letter, which sums up the argument on his side:

Dear Mr. Holt:

Apropos our discussion a few weeks ago about participation
in the milk situation, I am enclosing a copy of an editorial in

the *Journal of Commerce* a day or two ago, which quite likely you have already seen.

It seems to me to raise the old question of whether the church, as an organization, should go into politics and economics.

Several years ago I cut loose from the Chicago Church Federation, after making an ineffective protest, when it advocated the inclusion in the Illinois constitution of a limitation of Chicago's representation in the state legislature. I sympathized with the federation's purpose to secure better enforcement of laws against vice and liquor, but believed the proposed restriction to be violative of sound principles of self-government and certain ultimately to defeat its own purpose.

I have omitted of recent years all contributions to our Federal Council of Churches, because I was opposed to certain of its policies for like reasons. Without endorsing the enclosed editorial as a whole I feel constrained to concede that there is much justice in its criticism.

I have always been ready to get on with my fellow members of the Protestant churches on controverted questions of belief and practice, but if, in addition to the normal religious differences, one is to be under obligation if he takes his part in the organization to fight for his political and economic beliefs, and to accept, if he is to continue loyal to the organization, the conclusions of the majority of the church along political and economic as well as religious lines, it becomes a grave question whether one can adhere to the church.

The greatest bitterness against the Catholic Church has been caused by its interference with political matters. I think the Catholics have interfered less of recent years. It seems to me the Protestant churches are now taking over the very policy of which they complained so bitterly a few decades ago, and which they still resent on the part of the Catholics.

I regard it as the religious duty of every church member to enter vigorously into such political and economic activities as his conscience dictates. I cannot believe, however, that the church as an organization should take part in economic and political controversies.

Some of my reasons for this view are set forth in the enclosed editorial. In addition to the principle involved, there is the practical consideration that participation in politics by the churches is bound to excite general opposition and hostility, which I believe will do great harm to the cause of religion.

The editorial in the *Chicago Journal of Commerce* which accompanied this letter read as follows:

The Federal Council of Churches of Christ has recently issued a report which demonstrates in the clearest light the degree to which the council is meddling in matters which it ought to keep its hands out of.

The Federal Council has meddled in local matters, in national, in international; it has gone beyond the prohibition question into other questions of social legislation; it has taken a stand on the American naval question and on various international subjects; its president, Bishop McConnell, has become president of a nation-wide organization to induce the American states and the federal government to adopt the European system of old age pensions; and recently the council has issued a detailed report of several thousand words dealing solemnly with (of all things!) the "economic relationships existing between the dairy farmers in the Chicago 'milkshed' and the milk distributors, the dairy employees (milk-wagon drivers) of Chicago, and the municipality itself."

There is simply no limit now to the kind of public question which the Federal Council believes lies within its jurisdiction. The line between the things that are Caesar's and the things that are the proper province of the clergy is entirely disregarded by the Federal Council of Churches.

Such clergymen as Bishop Charles Fiske of central New York have for several years been declaring that the church ought to cease meddling in social and economic affairs in which it lacks knowledge and therefore lacks authority, and ought, instead, to confine itself to its ancient business of making good men. But the Federal Council entirely disregards such admonitions; indeed, it goes further — it issues contrary admonitions of its own; as witness an article in the February number of *Current History*, in which the Federal Council laments that there are still many ministers who " have not given themselves energetically to the social and economic struggle for the lives of the hard-pressed masses of the population."

Reading this lament, one would think the United States was a sad, backward country of eastern Europe, instead of the country with the greatest total of prosperity, and the greatest diffusion of prosperity in the world today, or in all the history of the world! The Federal Council has taken over the thought-habits and the very phraseology of European advocates of radical social reforms, although conditions in this country are sharply different from those abroad. Thus adopting the thinking and talking ways of European social reformers, the Federal Council is devoting itself to the task of putting European social reforms into effect in this country — one of these reforms being the old age pension, the enactment of which, as has been said, is being advocated by a national organization whose president is the president of the Federal Council of Churches.

In its wordy and banal report on the price dispute in the Chicago milk district, the Federal Council issues alibi after alibi for meddling in this matter. "First," it says, "the churches exist for the purpose of securing a ' more abundant life ' for men, women and children. It should be perfectly obvious that any effort in that direction is severely conditioned by the physical well-being of the people whose lives we would spiritually enrich. If ' daily bread ' is a legitimate subject for spiritual concern, daily milk is not less so."

The bald absurdity of the last sentence quoted is astonishing. In that sentence the Federal Council says in effect that because we ask " our Father in heaven " to " give us this day our daily bread," it is the duty of God's ministers to see to it that we get our daily bread, our daily milk, our daily everything else, and get it in exactly the manner and through exactly the economic relationships that they think wise. Probably never in history has there been a more preposterous perversion of Scripture.

In further excuse for its meddling, the Federal Council says, " Many Christians are coming to feel that the supreme test of the Christian church is not the number of adherents it can enroll under its banner but its ability to transform and refashion the world in accord with its ideals."

Thus the church is to interpose in every mundane matter, ranging from the League of Nations to the Chicago milkshed dispute. And this is exactly what the Federal Council of Churches has done. It has engaged in superficial studies of the Chicago milkshed problem, and has issued a wordy and superficial report. It has promoted conferences at the Chicago Theological Seminary, at which was discussed the high theological question of milk distribution. " The whole issue," says the council, " was dramatized in a play given at one of the conference sessions by the Seminary Players, entitled ' Milk! ' " The whole issue might better be summed up in the word, " Bosh."

It may seriously be asked: Does the Federal Council contemplate any limit to its interposition in social, economic and governmental affairs? Apparently it does not. Does it then think it can safely meddle forever? Danger lies ahead. The Federal Council is pursuing a mad policy. Any church or organization of churches that attempts to dictate the whole character of American government and American society will eventually be put under government regulation. That is the goal that the Federal Council is unconsciously aiming at.

To this letter and this editorial I made the following reply:

If I have been slow in writing the more formal answer to your recent letter about the participation of the church in controversial social questions, it is not because the matter has not been receiving from me the serious thought which your letter deserves. Unfortunately I have not succeeded in condensing my statement as adequately as you did, but I trust that it is still short enough to merit a busy man's attention.

Any discussion of the issue raised by this editorial and letter must deal as you say with the historic policy known as the separation of the church and state. I accept the principle without reserve. We are in a period when all the major social institutions have entered into their moral majority and are to be so treated. Institutions like the state, the home, the school, the professions and the trade associations are entitled to ethical autonomy. The churches have claimed the principle of autonomy for themselves and they have accepted it as a working principle for other institutions. But the emphasis on autonomy is not to the extent that each institution may go off and set up a social order by itself. Some time in the last century we rejected the principle of laissez faire as a working principle. Our ideal is rather a fellowship of free institutions governed by a common body of opinion which all help build.

Professor Cobb in his notable book, *The Rise of Religious Liberty in America,* pp. 15, 16, states the points essential to the policy of separation of church and state:

" 1. The civil power has no authority in, or over, the individual or the church, touching matters of faith, worship, order, discipline or polity.

" 2. The church has no power over the state to direct its policy or action, otherwise than its influence may be felt in the persuasion of the public mind toward the principles it teaches.

" 3. The state cannot appropriate public money to the church, or for the propagation of any religion, or any particular form of religion.

" 4. The church cannot look to the state for any support of its worship or institutions, otherwise than, like all other corpo-

rations, it may appeal, and must submit, to legislation and
judicial decisions in matters of pecuniary trusts and foundations, the ground of which legislation and decision is not at all
religious, but strictly civil.

" 5. The civil power cannot exercise any preference among
the various churches or sects, but must hold all as having equal
rights under the law, and as equally entitled to whatever protection under the law circumstances may furnish a need for.

" 6. The civil power may not make any distinction among
citizens on account of religion, unless the following thereof is
dangerous to society. Neither the right to vote nor to hold
office is to be invalidated because of opinion on the matter of
religion. Nor, again, is a citizen's right to bear witness or to
inherit property to be called in question for reasons of religion."

Now it is my contention that nothing has been done which
is out of harmony with paragraph two of Mr. Cobb's statement
which gives the church the right to make its influence felt in
the " persuasion of the public mind toward the principles it
teaches." In fact, I think that when the modern church establishes a research bureau with a trained staff of workers to gather
the facts which are vital to its programs of human brotherhood, it is in direct line of succession to the church which established colleges and in those colleges placed departments of
economics. Is there any difference in principle when Dr.
Timothy Dwight discusses Jeffersonian policies in Yale College and Ernest Johnson discusses Bolshevism in the " Information Service "? I think from all I know that Johnson is
probably the better trained man. Both were attempts to influence the public mind and both were in institutions designed
for that purpose by the church.

One approach to the validity of this procedure can be made
by noticing the importance in the modern world of this in-
tangible reality we call the " public mind." In a democracy
the public mind is king over all. It governs political policies,

it decides whether a given business will thrive or die. So important is standing room in the public mind that business organizations spend millions of dollars in advertising which can be considered as the attempt by written page or otherwise to create a public mind favorable to themselves. If a public mind is being created it would seem that the church ought to be held responsible for the spiritual and ethical quality of it. If a public mind exists which is out of harmony with the Christian mind the church has the right to be concerned about it. To expect the church to allow this public mind to be built along lines out of harmony with itself and never utter a protest is expecting what ought not to be. The church is legitimately concerned with the ethical phases of public opinion.

The next question must concern the nature of the question of the city's food supply — whether it is legitimately a matter of ethical investigation. I think you will agree with me that because of its very great importance to public welfare the public opinion which governs the city's food supply ought to be free from ideas which are unworthy. For instance, when the health commissioner announced last year that " Chicago had the purest milk in the world and the price of milk had not been raised to the consumer " the assertion was more than a mere pronouncement in the department of public health. It carried the warm glow of ethical triumph. As such it comes into the realm where it is right to ask, " What had been the cost of this pure milk to those who produced it? " The state some time ago took the ground that the clothing supply should be judged by its effect on the lives of the workers — the sweatshop was abolished by laws; likewise we have forbidden child labor in the factories and I think in every case ethical considerations are involved. Certainly we have the obligation to look behind our food supply to discover its effect on the producers.

But the question may very well arise as to the competency of the church to pass on such questions. Would it not be better for the church to confine itself to the old unquestioned

moralities about which even the best of us need perpetual re-
assuring? Ought not the church to leave alone questions where
there can be difference of opinion? As to the competency of
the church to speak on such questions, the following considerations are to be urged. The church is a widespread and very
delicate organism. Nothing happens in society which does not
register upon it. I was pastor of a church for five years in a
steel mill town and I knew in a perfectly legitimate way as
pastor of a church certain definite facts about the steel industry. I knew, for instance, the social effects of its employment
and wage policy. If there was no surplus income nor leisure
time there was no church since the church was built out of both.
I knew the by-products of the steel mill in terms of widespread
human attitudes. The Poles, for instance, hated the Negroes
who were displacing them in the labor turnover.

But someone will say, although these existed for me as problems they would not justify me in passing judgment upon
them. Here I think another consideration comes to the front.
The authorities of the steel mills were taking the initiative with
monthly pronouncements in informing the public about the
steel industry; they sought to inform us about the good points
of that industry but they did not say much about the weakness
which we pastors saw. Some of us thought a false public opinion was in process of forming. Judge Gary said he worked
fourteen hours a day on the farm and the implication was that
the twelve-hour shift in the steel mill was a good thing. But
in communities where there were twelve-hour days and seven-
day weeks, there were no churches and this constituted a condition in which the church had a right to be interested in the
same way that inadequate income in the milkshed made the
support of rural churches impossible. If the pastors thought
this could be remedied, I think they should call public attention to it.

One more consideration should be mentioned here. In pre-
senting its conclusions I think the church should distinguish

between those questions about which there can be a legitimate difference of opinion and those moral certainties about which all agree. Some matters ought to be presented at meetings where there is opportunity for discussion, like forums and adult discussion groups. They ought not to become a part of the service for morning worship whose function is to unite. Furthermore in an attempt to influence the public mind the church must use only persuasion and never try to bludgeon by appeals to fear.

The question will be raised, as in the editorial, Does the church propose to pass judgment on every issue? I do not think so, although I think it reserves the right to do so. Here I think it is a question of the urgency of the occasion. The church does not establish a college or a hospital when the situation is otherwise well taken care of. It much prefers to see vocational and political groups exercise their own ethical autonomy.

Furthermore a distinction should be drawn between the control once exercised by the Catholic Church and any control which a present Protestant church can exercise or is trying to exercise. Fighting for moral causes and fighting for the old ecclesiastical control are two entirely different affairs and should be recognized as such.

The question then comes to this: Are there areas of interest in the public and private order when the church can qualify as a critic? This goes back to the question whether there are moral issues which are so essentially a part of the public question that public policies cannot be settled apart from them. In such cases the church ought to be allowed to sit at the " cabinet table " and its judgment ought to count in the total public opinion which prevails.

Now what will be the probable results of such a course of action on the part of the church? I think the results can be contemplated with hope and not with fear. I believe it will promote peace and not strife. Let me illustrate in the case of slavery. There was a time in the early years of the last century when all the churches were declaring that slavery was wrong. Had the churches pursued the policy and spirit of John Woolman, who went about deliberating with his Quaker friends until all of them voluntarily liberated their slaves, our country would have been saved the terrible ordeal of the Civil War. John Woolman and the Quakers combined in themselves the technique of a true Christian procedure, a technique which the modern church is trying to revive. Unfortunately we do not adequately emulate him, but the fact that we do not only argues that we should improve our method. It is needless to say that there is nothing of dictatorship in such methods. The church would seek to educate and not to exercise lordship. It would appeal only to that court of true reasonableness before which all national and social policies must accredit themselves. Its authority does not extend beyond the rational character of its cause.

Now I am not insensible to your point that the policy will add to those forces working for the " dispersion of Israel." If theology now separates, how much greater will be the separation if we add social and political reasons for disagreement. Of course, another type of strain in the church might neutralize the theological strain. I once had a horse which was afraid of automobiles and streetcars and always shied when he met one; one day, however, he got caught between an automobile and a streetcar and went straight. I do not believe that the policy will dismember the body of Christ provided we have faith in one another's sincerity and exercise the manners common to good social intercourse. I have a picture of a church which is a fellowship of those who seek the Kingdom of God. It is a fellowship in which the binding tie is comradeship in exploring. I believe such a church will best conserve even the values which are now most precious to us.

Trouble in the milkshed did not subside. (For this I am very thankful. The kind of solution which would satisfy many people is one that they ought not to have. They would like pure milk from contented farmers — the sort who would work their wives and five children twelve hours a day in the fields and cow barns.) Nevertheless, in spite of criticisms such as were embodied in the letter sent to me, the committee kept on trying to think its way through the situation. The next group to descend on it were economists from the agricultural colleges and universities. They wrote long-drawn-out letters about the law of supply and demand and the liquidation of the inefficient under the capitalistic system. If they had read history they would have known that most of the planks in American democracy were put in place by farmers who talked about American rights and American standards of living. " What do you mean by justice? " a young economist asked me. " Justice," I said, " is something that a scientific economist doesn't know anything about."

The artists and the poets and the political scientists and the prophets know something about it. Gerrett Beneker, an artist, went into the steel mills and painted typical men. He chose men who he said would " knock hell " out of you if you didn't give them justice. The political scientists know that Americans are the kind of human beings who, every so often, " knock hell " out of present institutions because they do not get justice. When the economist gets caught in such a social shift he rubs his eyes, makes some caustic remarks about these " damned social reformers " and tries to collect on his accident insurance.

There is just one fact with regard to the way the city gets its milk supply about which I am very certain. The ultimate court of appeal is not the law of supply and demand. It has not been so since the city fathers passed a law saying that the individual citizen must not keep a cow

or a goat in his back yard. The law of supply and demand
did not determine who should belong to the milk wagon
drivers' union; there were fifty thousand men in the city
who could deliver milk just as well as the seven or eight
thousand men who did deliver it. The law of supply and
demand did not govern who should be the distributors
financed by two great banking firms in New York city.
Patents, tariff laws and willful combinations had much to
do with all this, as well as the law of supply and demand.
There was a law of common consent, rooting back in what
men thought of themselves and their neighbors, which
was always more powerful than the law of supply and
demand.

The problem of how a great city got its food supply was
fascinating because there were so many angles to it. So
many people approached the problem, each with his own
variety of assumption which rested back on what might
be called for that person an absolute. There was the point
of view which could be classified as urban. It always interested me how many times the *Chicago Tribune,* the So-
cialist party, the settlement workers and the Consumers'
Cooperative took the same point of view. Then there
were those who advocated the use of force. One morning
the farmers stopped all milk traffic to the city on highways
and railroads and the teamsters' union had control of the
streets of the city. The governor called out the National
Guard, but as one farmer said, " Just watch the National
Guard milk the cows." The only justification for force is
that advocated by Gandhi in his hartal: it is the only ges-
ture a big, inert public can understand, but it is a frail
reed on which to rest.

Among the farmers were those who appealed to the state

as over against the city. They would go to Springfield and organize the rural vote against the urban vote. Essentially theirs was an attempt to settle the price of food by majority vote. Majority vote is, for many, the modern absolute. The average Chicago man always looks under the bed to discover whether some farmer from downstate is lying in wait to rob him. The farmer does likewise. We have government by hallucination in Illinois.

Then there were those who professed confidence in the dictator or in the solution of laissez faire, both equally hopeless. The milkshed oscillated between poverty and affluence and the little children went hungry.

I finally came to the conclusion that the agreements by which a modern city gets its food supply constitute major problems in regionalism and demand a basic solution in ethical attitudes. Regionalism assembles between rural and urban forces a set of tensions which can be resolved by a sense of conscious unity and collective thinking, like all the other agreements by which human beings do together what they cannot do by themselves. Regionalism is the lineal descendant of the old town meeting which united town and country in conscious unity for collective thinking.

Millions of people could have a food supply provided they all recognized that this process must exist for all concerned — the producers, the consumers, and those who were in between. The accomplishing of this realization was largely a matter of education in attitudes and technical knowledge. One of the most interesting facts we discovered was that the farmers in the milkshed who were members of churches showed a larger willingness to rid their herds of tuberculosis in order that the city might have pure food than those who were not. The twenty-nine per cent who were church members furnished forty-two per cent of those who tested their cattle before city and state forced them to do so.

Millions of people could have their food supply provided they were willing to make war on special privilege which is based on certain assumptions about rights arising from force, property ownership, majority votes, state laws and city laws, government tariffs, transportation rates and combinations in support of some special interest of the producer, consumer, labor or capital. It was the will to special privilege which had to be fought. The desire for special privilege rooted in two sources, greed and fear. The assumption that all others were selfish immediately induced selfish organization on the part of those making the assumption.

Millions of people could have their food supply provided they were willing to take account of the naturalistic conditions governing that supply. There were reasons written deep in the ice age why the territory northwest of Chicago and not the territory southeast of Chicago provided the city with its milk. These reasons were but symbols of those reasons which developed as new ways of transportation developed and new ways of preparing a food supply were devised. Here was the legitimate field for all that the scientist had to say about the law of supply and demand.

Millions of people could have their food supply if they could have the chance to think and act about it as a community organized around that special problem. The argument for regionalism seems to me to be right here. The milkshed of a great city is a region of which a number of important groups are a part. These groups are partly in the city and partly in the country. The unity of the process ought not to be broken by the artificiality of city limits or state lines. If there is to be democratic or intelligent action there ought to be a certain kind of autonomy of this particular community. This ought to be accomplished without destroying organization which has its own justification for other purposes. The old New England town and modern regionalism have this in common: they bring town and country together for conference.

Finally, it is foolish to brand those agreements by which a great city gets its daily bread as of no ethical significance. They are not just secular. They are not just a part of the " scandal of capitalism." Most of the same old problems will arise under any " order." Communistic societies still face the problem of how many pairs of shoes shall be exchanged for a bushel of wheat.

The letter I wrote to my friend the prominent churchman of Chicago answers by implication the attacks now being made upon the various clergymen who, like those who participated in the work of the committee on the milk war, are taking a stand on major social issues, such as capitalism, fascism, democracy, war and race conflict. But as a matter of fact these clergymen are simply following the American tradition. There have been four great periods of social philosophizing in American history, and in every one of these periods the church has been concerned not only with private piety but also with the ethical phases of public problems. Those periods are: (1) The period of the theocracy, when men tried to establish and define a commonwealth founded on the Word of God and designed to benefit man; (2) the period prior to the election of

Thomas Jefferson, when the citizenship privileges of the United States were extended to the common man and the separation of church and state took place; (3) the period of the " roaring 40's " prior to the Civil War, when the issues were the freeing of the slaves and the preservation of the Union; (4) the present time, when the issues are the social control of capitalism, international and interracial peace, and the preservation of democracy. The church was not silent during the first three of these periods, nor ought it to be silent at the present time. For in a democracy there is supposed to be a rule of public opinion. We have given up hereditary monarchy; we do not believe in a totalitarian state; we believe in a government by public opinion, and no one group has a monopoly on that public opinion. It is true that democracy demands a functional separation between church and state, but that does not mean that a separate body of opinion should govern each.

That body of opinion which all of us help create and to which we must all give obedience is not to be monopolized by politicians, by business men, by the newspaper nor by the university. It has ethical phases which are of concern to the church and to which the church can contribute; therefore the church has a right in this field and should not be elbowed out by any group which claims a monopoly. The cry against preacher-politicians and preachers who " meddle in business " is the cry of those who desire to exercise monopolistic control over those areas and do not want to be bothered by any ethical issues which the church might raise. To be sure, the church is under obligation to be intelligent and to raise only those issues which are rightly to be considered questions of ethical import. But not to raise those issues at the right time and in the right way is simply playing traitor to civilization. The field of social criticism and social action, since it is a part of life, is decidedly the province of an organization whose Master claims control of the whole of life.

✦

It has been my contention throughout this book that from the standpoint of Christianity, that is a good social economy which when it is through with you leaves you a fit member for a spiritually mature society. It is from this vantage point that our contemporary social orders are to be judged. Are they, in their purpose, in their structure and in their general behavior calculated to evoke in human beings those attitudes which are consistent with ultimate spiritual growth? To be more specific: this standard demands that social orders induct people into the experience of increasing self-growth, reliance upon truth rather than force, the use of the imagination in determining what is good, capacity to associate with others in an experience of social faith, and a courageous belief in the ultimate triumph of spiritual values. Through these windows Christianity will look upon the present struggle of the social orders.

If God is working for spiritual maturity on the part of men then the Christian must work for it in terms of the social organization of men. God is a redeemer of persons and of peoples. The Christian will recognize a strategic significance in the primary relationships of life where the Christian ethic of love either finds its expression in filial devotion or is negated by all the ways in which people inside the family and neighborhood can exploit one another. The Christian will recognize that there are areas of sec-

ondary relationships where people deal with one another
on the basis of the cash nexus and where the Christian ethic
takes the form of honesty and fair dealing. There is a difference between the family and the market place. It is
futile to take the family relationship into the market place;
it is equally futile to try to treat all the people whom one
meets in the market place as one treats those inside the
family circle. Likewise there is a distinction between family relationships and those which are organized under what
we call political government. Here the relationship is one
of justice. We do not expect the judge and the policeman
to behave just as people behave inside the family. It is not
possible to draw a hard-and-fast line; nevertheless the virtues which are to be praised in a legislature are not necessarily the virtues which are to be praised in the parent. Yet
it seems the fair part to say that the Christian doctrine of
love is large enough to include all these relationships.

With reference to all social orders, however, the Christian must consistently maintain that they exist not as ends
in themselves but for God, whose ultimate purpose of love
must be the end of all society. This attitude calls for
judgment upon those social orders which set themselves up
as ends and which work to produce not spiritually mature individuals but dependent creatures whose only sense
of security is reliance upon some group or some human being who has assumed control over them. Christianity cannot praise irresponsible democracy nor totalitarian orders
which deny man the chance to be free. It rests on a firmer
basis. It brings its own order of values and independently
must criticize both.

Worship as Basic Self-Direction

In his book *Alone* Admiral Richard E. Byrd describes the experience of being lost and the process by which he found himself. He had advanced in the polar darkness beyond the series of bamboo sticks which marked the way to his hut hidden in the Antarctic ice floe.

. . . I was lost, and I was sick inside.

In order to keep from wandering still farther from the shack, I made a reference point. I broke off pieces of sastrugi with my heel and heaped them into a little beacon about eighteen inches high at the butt of the arrow. This took quite a little while. Straightening up and consulting the sky, I discovered two stars which were in line with the direction in which I had been walking when I stopped. This was a lucky break, as the sky had been overcast until now and had only cleared in a couple of places. In the navigator's phrase, the stars gave me a range and the beacon a departure. So, taking careful steps and with my eyes on the stars, I started forward; after a hundred paces I stopped. I swung the flashlight all around and could see nothing but blank Barrier.

Not daring to go farther for fear of losing the snow beacon, I started back, glancing over my shoulder at the two stars to hold my line. At the end of a hundred steps I failed to fetch the beacon. For an instant I was on the edge of panic. Then the flashlight beam picked it up about twenty feet or so on my left hand. That miserable pile of snow was nothing to rejoice over, but at least it kept me from feeling that I was stabbing blindfolded. On the next sortie, I swung the course thirty degrees to the left. As before, after a hundred steps, I saw nothing.

You're lost now, I told myself. I was appalled. I realized that I should have to lengthen my radius from the beacon; and in lengthening it I might never be able to find the way back to the one certainty. However, there was no alternative unless I preferred to freeze to death, and I could do that just as thoroughly a thousand yards from the hut as five hundred. So now I decided to take thirty steps more in the same direction, after scraping a little heap of snow together to mark the one hundred pace point. On the twenty-ninth step, I picked up the first of the bamboo sticks, not more than thirty feet away. No shipwrecked mariner, sighting a distant sail, could have been more overjoyed.[1]

Admiral Byrd had the problem of redefining his present and planning his future. Ours too is a pilgrimage into an unknown world and we must define our present and plan our future with reference to constants.

The primitive man's constants were his membership in a tribe or his relationship to a sacred place or law or person. Gradually sacred animals, sacred persons, cultural laws have been discarded. By a continuous refining of his constants and a continuous redefining of his relationship thereto, man has progressed in his pilgrimage to spiritual maturity. All the while man has been trying to find out what God is doing and to direct his own conduct on that basis. He does not pretend to sit up nights to keep the universe running; rather he seeks to come to terms with the universe, to guide himself with reference to those constants of whose significance he has become assured. Primitive man had a technique for keeping in touch with his constants. He invented elaborate rites for propitiating and cajoling the gods who represented the unalterable elements in his world. But just as the concept of the forces which control life was refined, so also was the method of maintaining relations with them. Modern worship is not intended as an attempt to influence the purposes of God, but rather as a technique for understanding them. It is a basic act in self-definition and self-direction.

The worship experience is not unlike the experience of the aviator who takes readings in order to pilot his plane to its destination. Howard Hughes said that he had been able to accomplish his flight around the world by maintaining celestial correlations, and by communicating through the radio with the men who kept watch on the winds and clouds. All the aviators of the past, all the geographers and astronomers, contributed to the scientific knowledge which made it possible for Hughes and his companions to fly above the clouds, pick out those points in the clouds to which they wished to penetrate and then find the spots they sought. The world of transportation and communication is in many ways a universal society that speaks a world language. East of the West Indies lies the hurricane zone where are hatched the storms which so often make a seething cauldron of the seas and bring devastation to the coasts. There was a time when these hurricanes were terribly dangerous, but now, when one starts, the men who keep watch send out little messages that travel between earth and sky and carry word to all the ships and to the cities along the shore that the hurricane is moving in such and such a direction at such and such a speed. The ships turn to port or the ships turn to starboard, the people in the cities leave the streets and make their houses fast, and the hurricane passes over or by them, a great wind and a loud noise. It has lost its danger because it has been defined with reference to something. The equator, whether it was discovered or revealed, has become a constant for the world of conscious communication, a point of reference for the physical world, which makes it possible to chart the earth and the sea and indicate distances and directions. When the officers step out onto the bridge of an ocean-going ship and take their readings they are performing in one respect essentially the act which men perform in worship. They are defining their present and planning their future with reference to a constant which experience has taught them they can trust.

The personal and social world also has its constants, but they are of a different order. You cannot insult the equator or be forgiven by it. The equator deals with the sense of space, not with the problems which have to do with the vanity, the avarice or the desire for power of the individual or the social group. Only a person who can define causes, establish roles and judge behavior can be the focal center of a world of persons.

Professor Tausch, discussing the forces which establish standards for the great professions, speaks of the part played in the development of professional consciousness " by certain dynamic individuals whose personality has crystallized the organization about a central idea and who have inspired their fellow members with their ideals." These individuals, he says,

do not pose as moral reformers or pretend even to be professional leaders. But they illustrate in a way the historic truth which H. G. Wells stresses, that the traditional ethical systems pale into insignificance in contrast with the powerful social impulses set going by the great religions of the world, impulses which are generated largely by personal leadership.   Just so and only so can a profession achieve full self-consciousness of its ideals clustered about a respected and revered practitioner.[2]

I was at Durban, South Africa, on the day of George VI's coronation.   I shall never forget my emotional experience as I listened, over the radio, to that marvelous ritual which is so much a part of the British empire and heard the voice of the king speaking to his people, defining the role of an Englishman and the meaning of empire.   The king's voice became, in a very real way, the base line from which the British empire was defined.   Such definition is of the utmost importance to the empire, particularly to its more distant parts where men are lonesome, where they struggle to keep alive in their minds its pictures and symbols.   Out there one is never quite certain whether he is speaking to an Englishman in his individual or in his " empire " capacity, and it is rather necessary not to confuse the two.

One night in Mysore, India, I attended a state banquet for British army officials.   When they stood to drink a toast to the king, spurs and sabers clicking, glasses lifted, the toastmaster saying " Gentlemen, the king! " I had sensations along my backbone such as I experience only at significant times.   When the banquet was over we continued sitting at the table; and though the minutes lengthened no one made a move to rise.   Finally I heard one lady whisper to another, " Have you forgotten that you are the ranking lady tonight and no can get up until you have left the table? "   All the people in the hall were stopped from acting because one woman had temporarily forgotten that she was not just a person; she was at that moment fulfilling a symbolic role of the empire.

Human societies are based on this kind of thing. Societies do not decide their actions with reference to imaginary lines in the cosmic structure, but with reference to persons who can establish roles and discover, define and defend causes. All groups have their leaders in whom the group ideas are centered. In celebrating the leader the group makes real the fact of its subordination to someone whom it considers to be worthy of leadership and who gives it a sense of vocation in life. The same is true of the Great Leader who is celebrated in worship. By all ritualistic performances and meditation we define our present and take upon ourselves obligations for the future.

If man were not a creature of action there would be little need for worship. Since he is a creature of action he must continually prepare himself for action through this preliminary discipline by which, like an aviator or a ship's officer, he takes his readings with reference to life. The old orthodoxy which was convinced that a man was lost unless he thus allowed his will to be directed, was essentially right. In emphasizing this need, orthodoxy prepared the way for man's spiritual maturity. Otherwise men dare not advance from the security of the dust. It is just this ability on the part of each individual to take readings with reference to certain fundamental constants written into the structure of life that constitutes the difference between the man of custom and habit and the man who is on his way to spiritual maturity. Evangelical theology was right in emphasizing the conversion experience. Conversion is preliminary to independence of soul. The man who is converted is transformed from a creature of habit and custom or a mere member of a social group to an individual aware for himself of certain spiritual constants on the basis of which he can come to terms with what God is doing in the universe.

The truly religious man is justified in claiming to know God's purposes, though not all forms of religion come to the same conclusion. Some religions leave men the creatures of ancestral loyalties; some tend to give them fear instead of courage. Christianity however — and it is in the terms of Christianity that Americans speak — teaches a God, revealed in Christ, who calls men to a vocation which they find revealed in the life of Jesus. God and Christ, man and his neighbor, become the great constants with reference to which the Christian defines himself. His growth in understanding these constants is not entirely a solitary adventure. He joins with others and in mutual meditation and self-revelation, in comparison of experience and in collective meditation, he finds his way in the world. This association has become the collective worship of the church. Each week the church celebrates four thousand years of man's experience with reality through faith and love.

No greater tribute can be paid to the importance of the worship experience than the assertion that in worshiping man is doing something inherently injurious. Worship, say its critics, creates the closed mind, the enslaved mind, the " retreat from reality " type of mind. It must be admitted that there are types of worship which do all these things. That is why not all types of worship are equally valuable. Some types of religious experience increase man's tendency to bluff and to take refuge in cults of self-defense. But the very power of worship to harm indicates also its power to make for a sense of inward security and of life direction.

The importance of worship for the achievement of a sense of direction in life suggests the need of freedom of worship. Admiral Byrd tells how the compass on the tractors he used in crossing the ice barrier would not work because of the presence of the smaller magneto on the tractor. The conscience of men is often deflected from the true absolute by the drawing power of the false absolutes set up by the fiat of state or class or race. Freedom of worship does not guarantee that man will seek the true magnetic pole, but only as he has this freedom does he have a chance to seek it. Democracy offers man freedom in worship because it trusts the uncontrolled conscience to find the true absolute.

There is of course the question whether any religion with a historic revelation does not bind the consciences of men and leave them dependent and less than spiritually mature and ethically awake. The answer is found in the nature of the reality with which man seeks to make contact. If a man in worship is faced with a code or an institution to which he must conform, then religion is an opiate which keeps him in a state of bondage; if he faces a God who is seeking spiritual maturity on the part of his worshipers, then religion is the perpetual guarantee of creative living. The question then is, What are the constants in the Christian religion with reference to which man defines his present and plans his future?

The belief that man knows what God is doing in the world is the heart and core of religion. Anything which falls short of this is mere autosuggestion. The Hebrew people down through the ages were concerned with, and had a conviction about, what God was doing through them for the world. Their pilgrimage to spiritual maturity was a great experiment through which they arrived at certain conclusions as legitimate as the generalizations of the scientist. Just as the generalizations of the scientist about the nature of the physical world are not considered dogmatic provided they stand ready to give evidence on demand, so the generalizations of the Hebrews about the inward purpose and plan of the universe are not to be considered dogmas but rather the ripened conclusions that came out of experience.

For almost two thousand years Hebrew thought concerned itself with the refining of its concepts of the great constants for human behavior. Successes and failures demonstrated the rightness and the wrongness of certain theories of life. Certain distinct gains were made. Certain experiments were tried and did not need to be repeated. In the Hebrew laboratory, the power of a great personality to found a community was demonstrated. The prophets formulated the thought and vision of a community based not on race or on nationality but on ethical and spiritual qualities. The fallacy of a social order based on autocratic self-pleasing on the part of the rulers was also demonstrated, and the integrating, healing power of the principle of brotherhood was experienced by the Hebrews. Thus the way was prepared for someone who would gather up in himself the fruits of the Hebrew experience and lay the foundation for a social order founded on loyalty to a person.

Into this community Jesus of Nazareth was born. But there were other communities abroad, certain centers of compulsion and fear which furnished the dark background for Jesus' life. Rome had triumphed. She had imposed her political system on all the nations bordering on the Mediterranean sea. It was a system built up on the use of force and the appeal to fear. Roman arms made common cause with the local authorities in every annexed nation. To a people with traditions of freedom such as the Jews cherished, Rome's rule was hateful, foreign, alien, and to be endured only because the people feared to throw it off. That Jesus knew the hatred of the Jew for Rome is perfectly clear from his dealing with the captious question about the paying of tribute to Caesar. The question itself has no point if there does not lie back of it a great popular hatred toward Rome which made it dangerous for a man to advocate the paying of the imperial tax. The hatred of Rome was also reflected in the popular estimate of the publican, the official representative of Rome in the collection of taxes. He had neither social standing nor religious privileges.

Jewish hatred of Rome had finally found organization in the party of the Zealots which, like the Sinn Fein of Ireland, was pledged to Jewish independence and the realization of Jewish national hopes. Those hopes were dramatized in Jesus' life when Satan led him to the lofty mountain, showed him all the kingdoms of the world and offered him world domination on Satan's terms. This was the dramatic plea of Jewish opinion for a leader who should build another world kingdom wherein the Jew should occupy the place Rome held in the contemporary order.

Rome was one center of compulsion and fear. The other was a theocratic community, the decadent Judaism of Jesus' time. Judaism at its best was not a legalistic religion which terrorized men in order to force them to conform to its prescription. In the reconstruction days following the Exile, the ideal of the prophets, which envisioned men living together in brotherly relationships under the guidance of the spirit of God, had for a time been partially realized. But the priest triumphed in Hebrew life, and in the fight it made for the preservation of its customs against the Hellenism of Alexander the Great, Judaism became hard and legalistic. The Pharisees, like the Puritans of a later day, won a noble fight for religious freedom, but along with the victory they carried the intolerant temper which they had developed in self-defense against Grecian arms. So while professing freedom Jewish religion became a matter of petty laws, customs and forms imposed upon the people by tyranny and threats of social punishment. A religion which had once possessed wide outlook and a universal appeal was narrowed down until only a Jew with all the limitations of a Jew could enjoy its privileges.

Jesus has been called the chief revolt-leader of all history. He has been pictured as the leader of the proletariat, the revolutionary who sought to organize the seething forces of unrest in the Roman Empire. It is true that Jesus taught a profound doctrine of social justice, but he was interested in something more than the starting of a revolt. The verdict of Jewish history was clear against such a plan. A civilization which can stand alone is more than a reaction. It requires more than a revolt to maintain a permanently changed society. Jesus had drunk deep at the springs of Jewish idealism. He looked forward to a society in which love of justice was not content merely to rebel against injustice in others. He envisaged a community characterized by moral and spiritual independence gained through discipline more severe than that of scribe and Pharisee, one whose members had learned through self-criticism the art of being just and giving justice to others. With true social insight Jesus saw the coming disintegration of the hate-breeding Roman Empire. His criticism of the contemporary order was severe. That order was wrong in principle and therefore must ultimately break down.

And Jesus called them to him, and saith unto them, Ye know that they who are accounted to rule over the Gentiles lord it over them; and their great ones exercise authority over them. But it is not so among you; but whosoever would become great among you, shall be your minister; and whosoever would be first among you, shall be servant of all. For the son of man also came not to be ministered unto, but to minister, and to give his life a ransom for many.[3]

Abraham and Moses had been organizing centers in the old community. Jesus offered himself as the center of the new community. He would be the vine, others would be the branches. He would bind men to him by the strongest tie they knew — love and social faith. Society shot through and through with suspicion would find faith returning when men came in contact with him. Even in his death he expected to draw all men to him. The idea is startling in its simplicity. If one man could ruin the world, a personality such as Jesus could save it by becoming the organizing center of a new order. For those who were members of his community were held together by something stronger than force and fear. Because he was worthy of great trust he created faith in them, and they carried that faith back into the world.   The integration of the community began when they gave to him trust and loyalty.   They were not his slaves but his friends.

This is my commandment, that ye love one another, even as I have loved you.   Greater love hath no man than this, that a man lay down his life for his friends.   Ye are my friends, if ye do the things which I command you.   No longer do I call you servants; for the servant knoweth not what his lord doeth: but I have called you friends; for all things that I heard from my Father I have made known unto you.[4]

Jesus' community was a community freed from the old compulsion of heredity.   A man did not need to be a Jew in order to be a member of it.   The only foreigner was the bad man; every good man had a right to citizenship.

There come his mother and his brethren; and standing without, they sent unto him, calling him.   And a multitude was sitting about him; and they say unto him, Behold, thy mother and thy brethren without seek for thee.   And he answereth them, and saith, Who is my mother and my brethren?   And looking round on them that sat round about him, he saith, Behold, my mother and my brethren!   For whosoever shall do the will of God, the same is my brother, and sister, and mother.[5]

Jesus confidently expected that his new community, characterized by social faith, justice and brotherliness, would supplant the old community based on autocratic compulsion, fear and heredity.   He was not an idle dreamer.   He was the keenest of social thinkers.   He saw that communities founded on force and fear always develop within themselves the antipathies which cause them to disintegrate.   He saw how small communities, like that of the home which centers around a good father, grow strong and persist through all the vicissitudes of history. Could he not build a world community in which men would partake of the spirit of their heavenly Father? Such a community would indeed be founded upon rock, and all the floods and storms of time could not prevail against it. Because he believed in God he had utter confidence that God had called him to found such a community. In parable and story he set forth his optimistic convictions.

Another parable set he before them, saying, The kingdom of heaven is like unto a grain of mustard seed, which a man took, and sowed in his field: which, indeed, is less than all seeds; but when it is grown, it is greater than the herbs, and becometh a tree, so that the birds of the heaven come and lodge in the branches thereof.

Another parable spake he unto them: The kingdom of heaven is like unto leaven, which a woman took, and hid in three measures of meal, till it was all leavened.[6]

Jesus anticipated the ultimate triumph of his community because he saw that the old order was impossible. It could never develop anything but human hate and human hate is the negation of community life. His order alone was possible. It gave promise of joy, happiness, comradeship, a community of the spirit where there would be youth and freshness and growth, a brotherhood which men could never outgrow and which would be the crowning glory of the creative work of God the Father. But he never minimized to himself the cost of the new community. Continually he warned men against the fallacy of hoping to secure it at bargain rates. The price was high — self-control and moral maturity won by severe discipline of body and mind.

Now there went with him great multitudes; and he turned, and said unto them, If any man cometh unto me and hateth not his own father, and mother, and wife, and children, and brethren, and sisters, yea, and his own life also, he cannot be my disciple. Whosoever doth not bear his own cross, and come after me, cannot be my disciple. For which of you, desiring to build a tower, doth not first sit down and count the cost, whether he have wherewith to complete it? Lest haply, when he hath laid a foundation, and is not able to finish, all that behold begin to mock him, saying, This man began to build, and was not able to finish. Or what king, as he goeth to encounter another king in war, will not sit down first and take counsel whether he is able with ten thousand to meet him that cometh against him with twenty thousand? Or else while the other is yet a great way off, he sendeth an ambassage and asketh conditions of peace. So therefore whosoever he be of you that renounceth not all that he hath, he cannot be my disciple.[7]

The establishment of the new community called for men who loved justice enough to seek it for the sake of its faith-creating power in society. The Sermon on the Mount is a masterly exposition of this thought. Jesus begins his discourse with a recital of those who will initiate the new order. They are the people who hunger and thirst after righteousness, who are merciful and pure in heart. And these qualities are to be found chiefly among the meek and the lowly who have come to hate injustice because they have felt the iron heel of oppression. These are the salt of the earth — the people who will keep society from rotting.

What is the nature of the justice of the new order? It is not a mere matter of law. It is justice in imagination as well as in deed. For action grows out of thought. Men cannot go on feeding the seeds of passion in the imagination and stop short of garnering the fruits of passion in deed. Hence sin must be fought in the imagination stage if it is to be fought at all. If the new community is to be free from murder, murder must be dealt with before it bursts the bonds of the imagination.

Ye have heard that it was said to them of old time, Thou shalt not kill; and whosoever shall kill shall be in danger of the judgment: but I say unto you, that every one who is angry with his brother shall be in danger of the judgment.[8]

And if the new community is to be free from licentiousness, its members must be clean in imagination as well as in action.

Ye have heard that it was said, Thou shalt not commit adultery: but I say unto you, that every one that looketh on a woman to lust after her hath committed adultery with her already in his heart.[9]

The justice of the new community requires also freedom from falsehood. Its builders must tell the truth not because they have taken oath to do so but because truth-telling is a primary condition of social trust and faith. Public opinion is based on what men speak, and if they speak untruth it will be vitiated.

Again, ye have heard that it was said to them of old time, Thou shalt not forswear thyself, but shalt perform unto the Lord thine oaths: but I say unto you, Swear not at all.[10]

Nor can justice be maintained on the narrow basis of the law of revenge. The law of revenge creates a vicious circle of evil. It enslaves men to one another and eventually shakes the foundations of society. For the self-defeating law of revenge, Jesus substitutes his principle of love which takes the initiative without waiting for goodness on the part of other people. He holds before his disciples the thought of a love which is like that of the heavenly Father who " maketh his sun to rise on the evil and the good and sendeth rain on the just and unjust." [11]

Ye have heard that it was said: An eye for an eye, and a tooth for a tooth: but I say unto you, Resist not him that is evil: but whosoever smiteth thee on thy right cheek, turn to him the other also.[12]

Again, the new order will not directly concern itself with justice in the distribution of material goods. It will seek first of all the righteousness of God, confident that in a social order which has paid the price of a right attitude between man and man, all men can secure what they need to live. The maintaining of right relationships among men is the key to the solution of the problem of food and drink. And where right relationships obtain, each man will be conscious of a true self-respect. He will not give that which is holy unto the dogs or cast pearls before swine, but his self-respect will never prevent him from laying more emphasis upon self-criticism than upon the criticism of others. He will not be so intent upon finding the mote in his brother's eye as to miss the beam in his own eye.

To those who are willing to pay the price the resources of the heavenly Father are pledged. At their knock there shall be opening and for their seeking there shall be finding. The gate is narrow and the pathway strait, but it leads to wide uplands. Other prophets may promise that grapes can be grown on thorns and figs on thistles, but they are false prophets. He who would reap the fruits of a permanent community must plant the tree of sincere, wholehearted righteousness. For such a one there will be a true reward.

Every one therefore that heareth these words of mine, and doeth them, shall be likened unto a wise man, who built his house upon the rock; and the rain descended, and the floods came, and the winds blew and beat upon that house; and it fell not: for it was founded upon the rock. And every one that heareth these words of mine and doeth them not, shall be likened unto a foolish man, who built his house upon the sand; and the rain descended and the floods came, and the winds blew and smote upon that house; and it fell: and great was the fall thereof.[13]

To this vision of an enduring community founded upon the love of his Father in heaven, Jesus was obedient unto death. And in his death he became significant for all mankind. Jewish and Roman justice broke down in dealing with Jesus and in their breakdown revealed the need of a higher righteousness than that exemplified in either of them. Jesus not only brought into being the universal society, but defined it for itself, gave it both a foundation and a goal and taught it the ways of reaching that goal. What Abraham, Moses and Samuel were for Israel, Jesus became for the world-wide society of the New Testament.

Jesus was the first moral teacher to point men to the use of their imagination for social good. In a profound sense, he made the imagination the instrument of virtue. Not a single one of his moral precepts can be observed without

resort to the faculty for sympathy. When Jesus is asked
how one should treat his neighbor, he has but one answer:
" Use your imagination and put yourself in his place and
treat him as you would be treated." The early Christian
fellowship was a fellowship of the holy imagination.

It was a fellowship also which had a sense of vocation.
Jesus' great apostle Paul made a unique contribution to
Christian thinking in his continual references to " the
call," which is the essence of what the new member re-
ceives when he joins the new society. He has a new role
to perform and the codes of living grow out of his calling.
The role becomes more vivid for him as he explores the
meaning of the type of life he has to live now that he has
given up the old sanctions of race and class and sacred
place and has left behind him the casuistic legalism of
the old order. He is an emancipated person, living no
longer by rule of thumb. But he must not use his freedom
as an occasion for licentiousness. His is a freedom to follow certain great principles and thus to become an archi-
tect of a world-wide order.

The new principle is that of love. It is easy to turn this
thought into mere sentimentality. Jesus said that love
means all that law ever meant. The law had enjoined the
regular and systematic worship of Almighty God, respect
for parenthood, respect for human life, respect for the
spoken word, and absence of jealousy. Love means all
this plus a moral concern which uses the imagination in
discovering new applications for itself. Love is the liquid
fire of moral energy before it crystallizes into code and institutional behavior. It breaks up the old slavery of environment and the attitudes of others. If you will agree to
treat me just as I treat you I can make you absolutely my

slave. I will strike you and you will strike me; I will smile at you and you will smile at me. You are not free to determine your actions; the environment I create determines them. And when all its members follow the law of revenge society cannot stand but gives way to anarchy.

True love would break the vicious circle — the love that Paul describes in the thirteenth chapter of I Corinthians. Henry Churchill King calls this passage the classic definition of friendship. Without this love, he says, all other things are worthless. Speaking with tongues — most highly prized of all the spiritual gifts in Paul's day — mystery-solving knowledge, wonder-working faith, magnificent liberality, torture endured even unto death — none of these is of the slightest avail without genuine love. "God's whole redemption is to a life like his own, to sharing his life; and that life is love." [14]

Love is the dynamic of the Christian society. And out of it arises an experience of social trust which holds men together. In the end the question, How is society to be held together? must be answered. If men give up the cohesions of race and class, geography and nationality, what remains? There is a bond which binds more firmly and more lastingly than any of these, though it is less tangible. That bond is the unity of those who trust one another, who rely on that integrity which roots in the fact that all are loyal to a constant which demands trustworthiness of each. This is basic to any society which would advance beyond the beggarly notions of race and class, geography and nationality. In the society in which we now live it is probably more important than any of us realize. We think we rely on law and force. Actually we rely on our fellow men. The great mass of men have confidence in one another.

When that confidence goes something terrible happens in human society. People who trust one another can move mountains. They can make all necessary changes in society. They can use all the techniques of science to analyze an old social order and project a new one. People who do not have the cohesion of social faith are helpless in the face of individual need and social evil.

The society held together by love and mutual confidence might be described as a society of friends. One of the most notable of the Christian groups has chosen so to define itself. Someone has said that those who are fit members of this " league of friendship " are characterized by integrity, breadth and depth of personality, deep community of interest, mutual self-revelation and answering trust. Over against these stand the members of the kingdom of evil — that coalition of predatory forces which support one another and represent an organized will to destroy rather than to build. Professor Charles Merriam says that there are two Chicagos — the predatory Chicago and the Chicago of the builders. That is a thought once made vivid by Augustine when he spoke of the two cities, the City of Lust and the City of Love. The fate of the City of Love in the midst of the City of Lust is the fate of those who must accept a life of redemptive suffering.

Can the society of love extend its rule into the wilderness of a world controlled by other principles of conduct? It is easy to become pessimistic about the possibility. Nevertheless the jungle has been crowded back at various times and places. The traveler in India is impressed with the fact that every town of any size has its wall. There was a time when the space around every town was a lawless frontier where men murdered, robbed and committed rape.

Today most of the children of India grow up without ever experiencing such conditions. The walls are merely a reminder of an unhappy past. The life of the African native is not so full of fear as once it was. There was a time when he lived in terror not only of cosmic forces but of the tribe which dwelt around the corner of the mountain. Today fear no longer grips him. The social jungle is being cleared. Bad as the modern world is, the frontier under the rule of tooth and claw has been pushed back to the national boundary line.

It is not unthinkable that it might be pushed back farther yet. The Christian constants today operate chiefly in the private world. But that they alone can serve to guide society as a whole is becoming increasingly clear. The society they define is a comprehensible one, and the techniques for actualizing it are at hand. It is conceivable that the Christian constants could dominate business and politics, that these could take on the characteristics of a world society. Everywhere men are learning the lesson of history — that social orders predominantly based on force and fear disintegrate because of their own self-generated animosities. The chain has not yet been forged which can hold together men who hate one another. A social order based on trust, on integrity of thought and mutual self-revelation, held together in its great collective projects by confidence, making use of all the skills which science has to offer — such an order might extend itself into a world-wide reality.

The Christian constant for the world of personal and social relationships can be approached from ever new angles. It is not a fixed line like the equator; it is an abiding relationship between persons. There was a time when this relationship was conceived as one between a lawgiver and a subject, and its violation could be adjudicated by sacrifice; by sacrifice the law was vindicated and the center of the personal and social universe remained undisturbed. In the fullness of time, however, it was revealed that God was not a lawgiver who demanded obedience but a father who calls all men to fulfill the role of sons in a society of brotherly men, the cohesive power of which is greater than the cohesion of force and fear. In that revelation sacrifice on the part of men is replaced by forgiveness on the part of God. If God's purposes are revealed in Jesus, he seeks spiritual growth and maturity for all his children.

God is using one part of the universe to redeem another. Into the hearts of some he breathes the revelation of himself as love. These become the world's great lovers who toil with a passion which burns but does not consume. Around them history seems to organize as the filings collect around a magnet. Central in God's constellation of lovers stands Jesus Christ. The church is but the institutional extension of his person. It must accept his great act of self-identification and extend his passion throughout the world.

Into others God breathes a spirit of new understanding. Our reading of the great drama of a redeeming God is different from that of the Middle Ages, to which " the earth was but a mean stopping place, a wayside tavern of ill fame, on the way to these other worlds." [15] John Calvin taught men that there is significance in their earthly life. Their ways of organizing and performing their human vocations are important steps in the pilgrimage toward eternal life. L. P. Jacks sums up in modern terms the insight of Calvin:

If by "the world" we mean such things as parliamentary or municipal government, the great industries of the nation, the professions of medicine, law and arms, the fine arts, the courts of justice, the hospitals, the enterprises of education, the pursuit of physical science and its application to the arts of life, the domestic economy of millions of homes, the daily work of all toilers — if, in short, we include that huge complex of secular activities which keeps the world up from hour to hour, and society as a going concern — then the churches which stand apart and describe all this as morally bankrupt are simply advertising themselves as the occupiers of a position as mischievous as it is false. In the words of Principal Caird, "The proposition would be unintelligible unless it were false." If, on the other hand, we exclude these things from our definition, what, in reason, do we mean by "the world"? The alienation from church life of so much that is good in modern culture and so much that is earnest in every class is the natural sequel to the traditional attitude of the church to the world. And now the world takes deadly revenge by retaining the position assigned her and standing aloof from the church.[16]

Nor will we read the divine drama exactly as the early Puritan read it. We will agree with Cotton Mather that God is the redeemer of persons and of peoples. But in place of the divinely inspired legislation of the Old Testament we set a love which is more dynamic, if less definite. We do not know of a God who spares man the necessity of making great decisions which call for both courage and adventure. We have more confidence in the God whose will is revealed in nature and in history although we still believe that his revelation in the face of Jesus Christ is the purest revelation of himself. We believe that this God was active in the past and is active in the present. He reveals himself to his church, but through events in history he sometimes teaches his church a lesson which the church has forgotten or failed to learn. We recognize that the great lovers of history do not face a friendly world. The cross is still there to mark the conflict between the love of God and the world which he is redeeming.

NOTES

1 Byrd, *op. cit.*, pp. 117–18.

2 Carl F. Tausch, *Professional and Business Ethics* (New York: Henry Holt & Co., 1926) , p. 20.

3 Mark 10:42–45.

4 John 15:12–15.

5 Mark 3:31–35.

6 Matt. 13:31–33.

7 Luke 14:25–33.

8 Matt. 5:21–22.

9 Matt. 5:27–28.

10 Matt. 5:33–34.

11 Matt. 5:45.

12 Matt. 5:38–39.

13 Matt. 7:24–28.

14 Henry Churchill King, *The Laws of Friendship* (New York: Macmillan Co., 1910) , pp. 102–3.

15 Lewis Mumford, *The Culture of Cities* (New York: Harcourt, Brace & Co., 1938) , p. 61.

16 L. P. Jacks, " The Church and the World," *Hibbert Journal,* Oct. 1906.